WHAT TO CONSIDER IF YOU'RE CONSIDERING UNIVERSITY

WHAT TO CONSIDER
IF YOU'RE
CONSIDERING
UNIVERSITY

New Rules for Education and Employment

KEN S. COATES
BILL MORRISON

DUNDURN
TORONTO

Project Editor: Diane Young
Editors: Ginny Freeman Macowan, Bob Chodos
Design: Jesse Hooper
Printer: Webcom

Library and Archives Canada Cataloguing in Publication

Morrison, William R. (William Robert), 1942-, author
     What to consider if you're considering university : new rules for education and employment / Bill Morrison and Ken S. Coates.

Includes bibliographical references and index.
Issued in print and electronic formats.
ISBN 978-1-4597-2298-9 (pbk.).--ISBN 978-1-4597-2299-6 (pdf).--ISBN 978-1-4597-2300-9 (epub)

     1. Career education--Canada. 2. High school students--Vocational education--Canada. 3. High school students--Vocational guidance--Canada. 4. High school graduates--Employment--Canada. 5. Postsecondary education--Canada. I. Coates, Kenneth, 1956-, author II. Title. III. Title: What to consider if you are considering university.

LC1037.8.C3M67 2014   370.1130971   C2013-907433-3
                                                  C2013-907434-1

1   2   3   4   5   18   17   16   15   14

We acknowledge the support of the **Canada Council for the Arts** and the **Ontario Arts Council** for our publishing program. We also acknowledge the financial support of the **Government of Canada** through the **Canada Book Fund** and **Livres Canada Books**, and the **Government of Ontario** through the **Ontario Book Publishing Tax Credit** and the **Ontario Media Development Corporation**.

Care has been taken to trace the ownership of copyright material used in this book. The author and the publisher welcome any information enabling them to rectify any references or credits in subsequent editions.

J. Kirk Howard, President

The publisher is not responsible for websites or their content unless they are owned by the publisher.

Printed and bound in Canada.

VISIT US AT
Dundurn.com | @dundurnpress | Facebook.com/dundurnpress | Pinterest.com/dundurnpress

Dundurn	Gazelle Book Services Limited	Dundurn
3 Church Street, Suite 500	White Cross Mills	2250 Military Road
Toronto, Ontario, Canada	High Town, Lancaster, England	Tonawanda, NY
M5E 1M2	L41 4XS	U.S.A. 14150

CONTENTS

For our grandchildren:

William Griffin, Spencer Griffin, Victoria Griffin, Katie Coates,
Christopher Coates, Hazel Coates

Graeme Gibbons, Ella Gibbons, James Tosoff, Henry Tosoff, Quinn
Morrison, John Morrison, George Morrison

In the hope that they will make the choices that serve them best.

ACKNOWLEDGEMENTS

This book emerged out of the interest and controversy that surrounded the release of our last book, *Campus Confidential*, a work that explored the Canadian university system from the inside. As we discussed universities with Canadians, we were asked repeatedly, "What should we advise our kids to do?" or, from younger people, "What should I do with my life?", and specifically, "Should I go to university?" This book is our answer to the hundreds of such questions.

This book reflects the endless support and patience of our wives. We are blessed with nine children (Bill has four, Ken has five) and thirteen grandchildren (Bill seven and Ken six). We have written this book with the futures of our children and grandchildren very much in mind.

Our work has benefited from endless conversations with faculty members, students, administrators, parents, and employers. We apologize to them for our obsession with the subject. We also wish to thank Kaiti Hannah, Lorien Hughes, and Amanda Sampson, who read a draft of the book and offered valuable comments. What you see here, however, is the result of thousands of conversations, seemingly endless reading, and a great deal of discussion between the two of us.

Dundurn Press has been a joy to work with. Diane Young saw the potential in an established idea and helped us reshape it. Margaret Bryant, Director of Sales and Marketing, has shown us the importance of understanding our audiences. Ginny Freeman Macowan and Bob Chodos, our editors, have done wonders with our prose. We really appreciate Dundurn's faith in us.

It was thirty years ago, in the fall of 1983, that we first met at Brandon University and started to write together. Although we also write books on our own, and have other collaborations, this book is the twelfth we have written or edited together. We hope that this book, like the others, will find its audience, and we earnestly wish that young Canadians will find in it much good advice that will help them navigate what looks to be, for people starting out in life, an increasingly difficult future.

Ken S. Coates, B.A., M.A., Ph.D., Johnson-Shoyama School of Public Policy, University of Saskatchewan

Bill Morrison, B.A., M.A., Ph.D., D.Lit., (Hon.), Professor Emeritus of History, University of Northern British Columbia

INTRODUCTION

SO YOU'RE THINKING OF GOING TO UNIVERSITY

STOP! Stop right now before reading any further. Ask yourself three crucial questions:

- Why?

- Why?

- Why?

If you are wondering why we ask this question three times, it's because it is so vital for your future.

For those of you just finishing your secondary education, choosing your path after high school is one of the most important decisions you will ever make, perhaps *the* most important. It's crazy to do it without giving it serious thought. It's equally foolish to make it based solely on what other people want you to do, or think you should do. For better or worse, your decision will shape your future in dramatic ways. You need to think long and hard about it. That's what we want to talk to you about.

Going to university can be a good choice. But it's not a good choice for all high school graduates. For some, it can be disastrous — leading to debt, disillusionment, and failure. University is not the only good option open to you. Have you considered:

- Polytechnics?

- Community colleges?

- Starting a business?

- Working for a year or two?

- Travelling or volunteering?

- An apprenticeship?

If you're listening to the general chatter — particularly from parents, guidance counsellors, and politicians — you may believe that university is your only option. It isn't. For some of you, going to university will be a terrific choice that launches you on a path to happiness and prosperity. For others, it will be a totally wrong choice. Many students find out too late that they've made a bad decision, and end up back home by Christmas or the spring, poorer and sadder for the experience. Others will slog unhappily to the convocation finish line — only then to discover that they are ill prepared for the world of work.

Of course your parents are ambitious for you. They want you to get a job indoors in a comfy office. They don't want you to end up working outside an office doing a job that involves physical labour — unless, of course, you are working on some environmental or similarly prestigious issue. And, let's be honest, your parents also want you out of the house, preferably before you are thirty, with the money you need to launch into a good life.

For those of you who already have an undergraduate degree or who find yourselves feeling insecure about your current situation, you may be wondering what to do next. Perhaps the job you were dreaming of hasn't materialized. You wanted to be a teacher, but there are so many unemployed teachers in their twenties that it's impossible to find a teaching job. You are working in a Starbucks, not a high school. This wasn't why you borrowed $30,000 and spent four to six years in university.

Should you return to university to get a different, or advanced, degree? Should you go to a polytechnic or a community college and qualify for working in a trade? Something must be done: you are on the good side of thirty (but not by much) and your parents are hinting that they'd like to downsize their house. The choices you made after high school have not worked out as you'd hoped. Obviously, you cannot un-make them, but you *are* young enough to make a new choice.

Regardless of how you came to be making this decision, now is the time to make smart, informed choices. This book will help you make the decision which best suits you; it also will help you prepare to meet the demands of today's workforce.

AN UNCERTAIN FUTURE

The future is as uncertain as it has been at any time in the last 150 years. People do not have a clue about what's to come. Twenty years ago, the main things that now define your life — smartphones, Facebook, Twitter, instant messaging, sexting, on-demand videos, iTunes, and illegal downloads — simply did not exist. Twenty years from now, who knows? Right now, China is on track to become the world's largest economy. The United States is on shaky ground. India is on the rise — and the Philippines and Vietnam may not be far behind. Europe, once solid and reliable, is torn by financial crises and social tension. You should see how limited the job prospects are for young adults in Europe these days!

In this unstable environment, how do you prepare for a successful future? The knowledge economy? Those who talk about it don't really know if a university degree will give you a good career. That huge demand for skilled trades in the western resource economy? Don't count on it lasting forever. The coming flood of retirements that will create hundreds of openings for young people? Not with middle-class jobs disappearing so fast. At least, the experts say, the service economy will remain strong — but will it?

We live at a time of constant and dramatic change. No one really knows what lies ahead — not us, not your parents or teachers, not politicians or governments, and not the college and university recruiters. Indeed, the only piece of wisdom about which we have absolute confidence is this: no one knows how the next ten to forty years will unfold.

And yet, here you stand — ready to make the choices that will determine your future. Before you leap into it, you have some tough decisions to make. If you are about to graduate, you need to determine how you will make your way into the confusing, high-stakes world of life after high school. Your parents and guidance counsellors urge you to go to college or university. If you live out west, you might be tempted by a well-paid, low-skill job in the resource sector. You may be planning to leave home. (Be honest: Doesn't everyone want to be fully independent from their parents?) If you want to go to university, which one do you pick? And if you've already gone to university, did you make the right choice? Which program? Why not college? Are the polytechnics really different? How about an apprenticeship program? Or a year of travel or international work, or even volunteering? So many options, so many expensive choices, and so little guidance.

PREPARING YOURSELF: HOW WE CAN HELP

This is where we come in. We want to help you make a careful choice about your future. Whatever you choose to do will have upsides and downsides. It costs a small fortune to go to university — and the money is poorly spent if you drop out after a year (or sooner) or if you cannot find a decent job after graduation. We have watched too many students make too many bad choices over the years. We want to help you figure out what is best for you — for now and for the future. Time spent thinking and planning your future may well be the best investment you ever make.

As we proceed here, we will try to maintain an avuncular[1] tone — we'll keep it friendly and informal. We like universities and we like students. We wish both of them well, though we recognize that both have their faults. We also are fond of colleges and really keen about polytechnics, and we like well-planned travel, work, or volunteering. We offer ourselves as guides — two veteran university teachers who have been working with young adults for, well, a very long time.

Preparing for life after high school and university is a difficult and confusing task, for parents as much for the young adults heading off to advanced education or the world of work. We want to help. We have seen thousands of new students make their nervous way onto campuses. We have welcomed them to their first class at university, and have sat with them and their parents when their university dreams exploded in a welter of failed examinations, skipped classes, and poor essays. As parents ourselves, we have watched our children work their way through their studies. We know that there is nothing easy about what lies ahead. We have seen many students fail at university — and then succeed in life. We have watched young adults make foolish decisions that hounded them all their lives. We have seen people under-estimate the value of a college diploma and misunderstand the importance of work. We think we have some wisdom to share.

We should, however, confess: we are both old. One of us is moderately old; the other is *really* old. One of us got his BA in 1978 and other in (shudder) 1963. So, why should you listen to a couple of seniors? Let us ask you this: Do you want advice from some newcomer who just got out of college the day before yesterday, the ink on the diploma still damp, some dude who hasn't got over his last beer bust? Or, would you rather listen to two guys who've been in and around universities in Canada and all over the world (first as students, and then as teachers and administrators) for a total of nearly ninety years? There's not much we haven't seen and done at universities — and here we are giving you the benefit of all this hard-won experience. Go ahead: listen to this newbie next door, or to a couple of veterans. Your life, your choice.

We don't presume to tell you what to do, since the life trajectory of each family and every student is different. If you do choose to go to university, we can offer insights into how they operate, what typically happens to families and students in their first year, and how to get the most from a university career. But if you decide — as many of you should — to choose one of the various non-university options available to you, we can help you to be clear about your rationale and your prospects. Even those of you have already completed a course of study can, we think, benefit from what we have to offer.

Let us make this crystal clear: we believe that, for the right student, with the right attitude, a university education is an unbeatable experience and a fully worthwhile investment. If you are that student, your university experience will help you to develop valuable skills, gain insights into the human condition and the natural world, make great friends and life-long contacts, and emerge at convocation as a profoundly changed person. However, we also know that colleges, polytechnics, and apprenticeships are brilliant options for just as many students — and that time spent travelling, working, or volunteering can equally set you up for a very successful life.

In the chapters that follow, we are going to encourage you to consider *all* options — university, apprenticeship programs, colleges, polytechnics, entrepreneurships, religious and military colleges, volunteering, travel, and work — before making a decision about what comes next. Whether you are a soon-to-be high school graduate who can draw upon your parents to support you in this process or a young adult who needs to make a change, we are going to help you to think long and hard about the match (or mismatch) between your skills and interests and the choices you are considering. We will ask you to look deep into yourselves to honestly identify your desires, abilities, and work ethic to succeed in the demanding and largely unsupervised world that you're about to enter.

We have written this book to challenge you to look at the wide variety of options available to you — and not simply default to the one closest to home. For some of you, this process may affirm the choice that was already at the top of your list; for others, the outcome may be very different from what you expected. In either case, we'll have done our job, you'll have done your homework, and we believe that you'll be better prepared for what lies ahead.

CHAPTER ONE

THE CROSSROADS:
MAKING CHOICES THAT MATTER

ARRIVING AT THE CROSSROADS

So, you're reading this book because you have reached a significant crossroads in your life. Now is the time for you to decide what you will do next — and the options are many. Chances are, as a Canadian youth or young adult, you've heard that attending university is the only responsible choice you can make. That message — which underlies our family, entertainment, business, industrial, and governmental interactions — may well have been accurate for your parents' and grandparents' generation, but things have changed. If you're going to make the choice that is right for you, you need — first and foremost — to consider not only where we, as a society, *are* but also where we *are going*. In this chapter, we'll do our best to guide you through that consideration.

More than ever before, it must now seem as if everybody wants something of you. Your parents, of course, want you to be happy — but they also want you to be independent, employed (ideally established in a prestigious and rewarding career), and out of the house. Employers want you to be well trained (for the jobs of the present and future) and ready to work — very hard and with real commitment. And governments want you contributing to society and paying lots of taxes (mostly to support your parents and grandparents in their retirement, for which we thank you).

In much of the modern world — certainly in our world — achievement has become the exception rather than the norm. Ours is increasingly the world that Malcolm Gladwell describes, in *Outliers*, where he argues that the most talented individuals in any field must spend 10,000 hours practising to hone their skills to the highest possible level. How many do this? How many become masters of the golf course, or the operating theatre, or the concert hall? People such as Sidney Crosby and Serena Williams, maybe — but not many. But of course this was always true: there were never very many masters. If you are one of those truly stellar individuals, you are special — and, as long as you continue to challenge yourself, you are destined for a successful life.

Fifty years ago there were a great many people in Canada who worked hard at an early age to master difficult skills and meet a tough standard: studying Latin and preparing for the provincial examinations which were a prerequisite for high school graduation. Now, however, we live in an age where the pressure has been torqued back, where children are allowed to perform at their own level; if they think the task facing them is stupid or too tough, they are excused from trying.

Today's Canadian youth have the luxury of a more leisurely transition into adulthood. Our high school graduates are spared the high-profile, high-stress, "study for years until final examination hell" system that East Asian high school graduates endure. They are not pushed hard by their teachers. After all, students in Alberta were given a break when the province ruled that teachers were not allowed to assign zeros, even when students fail to complete an assignment (arguably one of the silliest ideas in a modern school system full of silly things). Most parents see it as their duty to insulate their teenage children from the challenges of adulthood, seeking instead to launch them gently into a confusing, complex, and surprisingly unwelcoming world.

That being said, we fully recognize that not all of you have arrived at this moment easily. Those of you who come from families living in poverty or family crisis, are moving from rural and remote areas, or are continuing the transitions of immigration have had very different experiences. You know only too well the realities of contemporary Canadian life; consequently, you will head into adulthood with your eyes wide open.

So, young person, why is everyone so worried about you? You are eighteen years old or nearly so, in the final semester of high school. You might be able to vote, enlist in the army, drive a car, drink, and otherwise act like an adult. You and your friends are tired of your parents, teachers, and guidance counsellors lecturing endlessly about university, colleges, and jobs. Although you don't like to admit it, you are nervous, too. If you aren't, you should be. It is hard to miss all the talk about the collapsing middle class, youth unemployment, government debt, climate change, and all the other things that just make you want to stay in high school forever.

THE WORLD AROUND YOU

It seems unfair, doesn't it? You are heading into adulthood at a very difficult time. Life may not be easy. Demographers claim you may have a lower life expectancy than your parents (too much junk food and too little exercise). The financial misdeeds of your parents' generation, compounded by the spending habits of the baby boomers, mean that you are inheriting huge obligations that will dog you for the rest of your lives. And those wonderful technological innovations — the ones that put a smartphone in your hands, that allow you to share movies and music for free (but not, we hope, this book) — are also transforming the world of work by eliminating more jobs than they create.

It wasn't so long ago that the rewards of graduating from high school were more or less guaranteed. Even those who didn't finish grade twelve could do reasonably well. As recently as the 1970s, there was a good deal of decently paid work to be found in the nation's factories, construction sites, fisheries, mines, and logging camps. A trades ticket or a college diploma was solid preparation for a well-paid life. A university degree was an even better ticket. Some of the country's major employers — Eaton's, Simpsons-Sears, the big banks, governments at all levels, the armed forces — hired for potential as much as skill and offered training and career progression for graduates from our universities.

Canada is a great place to live. We aren't as rich as Dubai or Macao, but in all of the top measures of the human condition that matter — life expectancy, infant mortality, literacy, educational attainment, distribution of income, safety, and the like — this is one of the top nations in the world. There is a reason why Canada is one of the leading destinations for immigrants and, as evidence of our national compassion, refugees as well. The country dodged a major bullet during the 2007–08 global financial crisis and is the envy of most of the world in terms of its government budgets and level of debt.

So, why worry? Canada has an enviable standard of living and quality of life, and abundant natural wealth. Despite issues that sometimes dominate media attention, such as the Senate spending scandal in the fall of 2013, our public institutions — Parliament, bureaucracy, courts, police, and armed forces — are among the most trustworthy, accountable, and honourable anywhere. Whatever the country's shortcomings, and these are obvious and not few, you are coming into adulthood into one of the richest, most peaceful, safest, and, dare we admit it, greatest nations on the planet.

There are some gloomy spots, of course. Aboriginal people do not share in the nation's prosperity, particularly if they live in isolated communities. There are pockets of real economic hardship across the country: one-industry towns without an industry, rural and remote communities that offer few economic opportunities, once-thriving fishing communities destroyed by the decline of coastal fisheries, and working-class segments of industrial cities that are now pock-marked by abandoned factories. Many new Canadians, including thousands with diplomas and advanced degrees that are not recognized by Canadian employers, struggle to find secure and decent jobs. All countries have pockets of economic distress and Canada is no different, but we do offer various government support programs to ensure that even people without work have some measure of support.

Another part of the problem rests inside Canadian companies. Over the past few decades, Canada has lagged behind other industrial nations in productivity and competitiveness. Put simply, Canadian workers and companies do not produce as much per unit of work or input as do our main competitors. In the past, Canadian factories operated behind substantial tariff walls that gave domestic companies a substantial financial advantage over firms from other countries. They could be less efficient and produce items at a higher cost than other countries and still sell more cheaply in the Canadian market. However, in the era of the North American Free Trade Agreement, the recently signed Canada-EU Trade Agreement, and freer world trade where lower-cost foreign goods compete directly with Canadian manufactures, inefficiency and low productivity leave Canadian companies behind.

One reason Canadian firms are uncompetitive is that this country under-invests in new industrial technologies. Canadian firms are not particularly innovative and do not purchase new labour-saving and labour-enhancing equipment at the same rate as their American counterparts, to say nothing of the robotics-obsessed Japanese and East Asians. This is one of the classic double-edged swords of the twenty-first century: on the one hand, to stay competitive and to hold on to market share in the hotly contested global market, Canadian firms have no choice but to invest heavily in new, cost-reducing technologies; on the other hand, these investments will cut substantially into jobs for the vast army of low-skilled, high-waged Canadians who have been central to this country's economic fortunes for decades.

Look at the pulp and paper industry, for example. With rich forests and hundreds of semi-skilled workers to keep the plants operating, Canada's paper industry was thriving; now that they rely far more heavily on highly mechanized processes, a once-significant job market has been greatly reduced.

Much the same is going on inside the country's professional offices. Firms are changing in dramatic ways: more compact corporate structures with fewer middle management positions, much less emphasis on developing professional staff over time, a sharper focus on staff with specialized technical or management skills, greater reliance on contract workers, fewer employees, and a willingness to out-source portions of work to other countries. Tax forms, medical charts, diagnostic x-rays, scientific results, and many other functions are increasingly being done outside the country. The big exception to this, not surprisingly, is government — which has grown faster than our prosperity and even faster than our population.

Your grandparents and, to a lesser extent, your parents lived in a world of loyalty — of employers to employees and of workers to their company. That sense of loyalty rarely exists today. The contingent workforce — a fancy term for people (often with advanced skills) who move around between companies in the same sector — is growing fast. When your grandparents and parents talk about the world of work, they are often referring to a time when career-long employment was the norm — rather than the exception — and when employers focused on developing the potential of individuals over the long term. This is not your world.

For the last decade or more, political leaders have been touting what they call the "knowledge economy." The world of work, they thought, was going to require at least fourteen years of education (elementary school, high school, and college or university). It made sense, on the surface, and it was so much cooler to talk about than what we might call the old "sweat economy." This was the world of Nortel (for a time), Open Text, BlackBerry, Disney animation, eBay, Facebook, Google, and the like. So the message pushed aggressively by former Ontario Premier Dalton McGuinty (the "education premier") and American President Barack Obama made intuitive sense — and parents and young people responded to the simple and compelling message.

The knowledge economy turned out to be largely an illusion, however. True, the high-technology sector needed skilled personnel. People with credentials in computer science, electrical engineers, and animation found ample opportunities. Those without specialized skills found themselves with many fewer job offers, lower incomes, and much less job security. As it turned out, Canada ended up with a combination of the knowledge economy and the old economy (resource development and old-style manufacturing — the former booming and the latter in free fall for quite a while). The so-called new economy was a rapid expansion of the service economy — as opposed to the anticipated economy of fancy high-tech work. Hundreds of new jobs emerged in the finance sector — high-paying work with banks and insurance companies — creating excellent opportunities for accounting, finance, and commerce graduates. But the real growth in employment came in the service industries: health care, restaurants, hotels, travel, recreation, fitness clubs, and personal care. Most of these jobs, in contrast to the lofty promises of the knowledge economy, required little specialist education or training, offered little job security, and provided only modest incomes.

HOW THIS AFFECTS YOU

So how does all of this affect you? You aren't reading this book to learn about the work environment of the 1960s. You want to get information that will help you make choices that will serve you well throughout the rest of the twenty-first century. So, let's bring it closer to home. It helps to start with the tough bit. Canada's young adults have been raised with extremely high expectations. Many carry these expectations about work, education, and lifestyle with them as a guarantee about their future.

Expectations and realities, however, will not necessarily match. There are many warning signs that the future is not likely to be as easy as most young Canadians have been led to expect. Although there is a great debate about the trajectory of Canadian life, certain things seem evident:

- many young people will not be more prosperous than their parents,

- the high cost of real estate will postpone home ownership for many,

- university and college debt will hang like a financial albatross over an entire generation,

- the public debt run up by parents and grandparents will shackle governments for decades to come, and

- health care costs of the elderly will add to the tax rates that today's teenagers will pay down the line.

Thanks to the globalization of our economy combined with techno-logical innovations, mechanization, and corporate restructuring, there is even more bad news:

- many of the jobs everyone thought would be waiting for today's youth have been out-sourced to other countries;

- readily available secure, decently paid blue-collar jobs, widespread unionization, and middle-management opportunities have given way to a world with fewer middle-management and more part-time jobs, largely union-free workforces in the private sector, and heightened specialization;

- major national firms, such as the Hudson's Bay Company and Eaton's, and even new-economy firms, such as Nortel and BlackBerry, have either disappeared or cut back on employment opportunities.

The crucial difference between the prospects facing today's youth and the world of their parents is that easy avenues for advancement and prosperity are becoming much rarer. High-wage, low-skill work abounded in the country's factories, construction sites, and mining and logging camps. University graduates, regardless of field of study, attracted good salaries in a welcoming employment market. Skilled professionals — doctors, dentists, optometrists, engineers, and architects — typically had the choice of a variety of good career options. A vast range of middle-class work defined the country, permitting young Canadians to start families on a single income, buy a decent house in the suburbs, launch small businesses in prosperous small towns and emerging cities, or find a place in a rapidly growing civil service.

The situation is far from hopeless, as we will show later. There are good opportunities for talented, motivated, and hard-working young adults. The coming retirement of the baby boomers should create thousands of openings for the ambitious, or so the young generation has been promised. (Let's face it: if they refuse to retire, they can't refuse to die — much as they might want to.) The world has shrunk in ways previously unimaginable. Many of today's young people will find themselves working in Asia, Europe, or other parts of the world — or working for companies based in those countries or for firms selling to or working well outside Canada.

Opportunities for entrepreneurship abound; digital technologies enable anyone to build a business and to sell products or provide services to customers the world over. Resource companies working in the far North offer high wages and benefits, albeit for work that involves spending a couple of weeks in a remote camp before flying home for a week or two off. Entire new sectors — such as digital animation, social media, and e-commerce — have emerged in the past twenty years, creating great career prospects for the technologically proficient and creative. These opportunities are terrific, but the number of such positions is very small compared to the size of the national workforce. However, many more new avenues for personal and career growth will likely arise in the future.

But the sad truth is that, unlike the situation two generations ago, there will not be enough of these jobs to keep everyone in the middle. It won't be exactly like contemporary China — where the choice seems to be between a good education and the rice paddy — but it's heading somewhat in that direction. Some of you will find berths in the middle class, and some will not. Getting there will be harder than it was for your parents and grandparents. Once you arrive, your hold on the spot may be uncertain. But of course, if it was as easy as it was fifty years ago, you wouldn't need us, would you?

LEARNING EQUALS EARNING — OR AT LEAST IT ONCE DID

For most young people in Canada, attending university used to be like winning an express ticket to the middle class. Everyone knew what the prizes were: white-collar work, a decent salary, and proper benefits. With those prizes came the opportunities connected to financial security: marriage, children, a house, a car or two, and an occasional holiday in the sun. This, after all, is still what passes for the good life in Canada. This is still what young people want, and what their parents want for them. You will note that these aspirations tend not to include blue-collar work. Survey after survey of Canadians demonstrates the current preoccupation with escaping from working outdoors or making a living through physical and technical labour.

There was a time when a university degree delivered on its promise. Through the 1950s, 1960s, and 1970s, a university degree took a young adult to within reach of the brass ring — largely because there were far fewer university graduates per capita than there are today. The high school graduates who headed for university were better prepared to earn their degrees and then, having done so, had a very good chance of finding middle-class opportunities. The strong demand for government workers, lawyers, teachers, university professors, middle managers, and the like ensured that the vast majority of university graduates could, with comparatively little effort, find their way into a decent career.

Governments naturally thought that if the system worked for 5, 10, or 15 percent of the population, why not for more? Or, as has been suggested, why not for everybody? Why should a minority of the population get all the good jobs? Flushed with the success of university education, and believing wholeheartedly in the knowledge economy, governments throughout the Western world launched a huge expansion of the university system: new universities opened; women were recruited; new

Canadians and children from working-class backgrounds attended in large numbers.

The message was simple, and in those days it was largely true: *learning equals earning*. For decades, the university system promoted that equation, with an equally simple statistic: university graduates earned an average of $1 million more than high school graduates over the course of their careers. This statistic was more recently amended to $1.3 million over a high school graduate and $1 million more than a college graduate.[1] The claim, though statistically true, was always deceptive: it reflected average earnings, and was far short of a guarantee. Graduates in some fields earned far more than the $1 million premium; other university graduates earned considerably less. Still, it made for a powerful and simple plan: go to university, regardless of the field of study, and you will make a lot more money than those who do not.

NARROWING THE FIELD

Several years ago, a company in the Maritimes that hired large numbers of people each year to handle telephone calls placed a job ad which indicated a preference for individuals with a university degree. When questioned about the need for a degree for employees who doing a simple, unskilled job, a company executive explained that each year the firm looked for between forty and fifty people for these jobs, and received close to five hundred applications. Of those, at least 150 had a university degree. For the company, the degree requirement was simply a way of culling a long list down to a manageable short-list from which they could easily find forty to fifty decent employees.

CREDENTIALS MATTER

Credentials do matter — although not necessarily for the reasons that institutions, parents, and guidance counsellors think. The first benefit of a university or college degree or diploma, sad as it is to say, is the simple fact that it separates an individual from the crowd. As one cartoon caption said, "The easier it is to get a college degree, the dumber you look for not having one."[2] At one time, a degree was a mark of high distinction and spoke directly to motivation, ability, and specific skills. Now, in a situation where at least 70 percent of all Canadian high school graduates continue on to some form of post-secondary education (they don't all complete it), the primary advantage of a diploma or degree is that it indicates you are not one of those simply not able or willing to go to college or university.

So, a diploma or degree, if it does nothing else, can keep you on the list of candidates under consideration for entry-level, unskilled jobs. This won't make your heart beat faster. It isn't much of a selling point for university or college recruiters, but it makes sense from the company's perspective. In a nation awash with college and university graduates, using the degree as a means of winnowing the pile of applications makes perfect sense. After all, diploma or degree holders have invested two or more years and a good deal of money in their own development, and have shown a certain level of motivation. Most of them can read and write at a fairly high level.

This, then, is our first message: a diploma or a degree serves, at a minimum, as a means of separating people from the 30 percent of Canadian high school graduates who do not continue their studies, and from those who do not complete high school at all (still 13 percent of the adult population).[3] It is a barrier over which the really unqualified cannot pass. That doesn't say much though. A four-year degree is a pretty expensive way to distinguish yourself from a group that includes many under-achievers of various kinds.

THE EMPLOYMENT PARADOX

In many parts of Canada there is a rather curious paradox: they have *people without jobs and jobs without people.* A major study in Ontario revealed a large and growing number of unemployed people — including many thousands who are Aboriginal, have recently arrived in Canada, are living with disabilities, or lack an adequate education — who simply cannot find easy entry into the workforce and thus face years of unemployment, temporary positions, and low incomes. At the same time, and this was the surprise, Ontario businesses had hundreds of thousands of unfilled and unfillable jobs.

Many of these positions were in blue-collar work — the country has such a shortage of plumbers, pipefitters, and the like that companies are recruiting aggressively overseas. Many of the other vacant positions are in highly skilled, high-technology positions. In both cases, severe shortage of people with critical skills has slowed corporate expansion and interfered with economic growth generally. This problem is nation-wide, with similar problems in the booming western Canadian resource economy. Ironically, having hundreds of thousands of young adults coming out of colleges and universities with diplomas and degrees has not helped many companies find the people to meet their needs. Canada is not the only country facing this paradox: Mongolia, a for-mer Communist country that is joining the democratic and capitalist world, expanded its university system rapidly. Their resource economy has taken off. Their current problem? A shortage of skilled tradespeople and too many arts and science university graduates!

You can take an important lesson from this paradox: not all creden-tials are equally valuable in today's economy. Some degrees or diplomas provide the holder with only a minor boost in employment possibili-ties; the most promising opportunities (present and future) go primar-ily to people with specialized skills. In terms of job openings, income, and career security, accountants have a greater range of prospects than those of a generalist in biology or sociology. Nurses and doctors, in gen-eral, find opportunities that outstrip those holding degrees in business administration. The credentials do not reflect how hard it is to get the degree — getting a degree in philosophy is every bit as challenging as getting one in electrical engineering or marketing — but rather reflect the connection between the skills learned and the marketplace. Leading-edge companies, from digital economy firms in Waterloo to oil sands companies operating in Fort McMurray, require workers with targeted and very specific abilities — most of which need specialized certificates, diplomas, or degrees — followed by practical experience.

Unfortunately, this is the raw truth about credentials: there are no guarantees. Even the most carefully crafted life — one based on the right selection of high school courses, a thorough evaluation of degree or diploma options, successful graduation and an aggressive approach to job-hunting — is no assurance that a job, career, and income will follow in due course. The best opportunities will go, now and in the future, to people with the right credentials, exhibiting the right personal qualities, at the right time, in the right place. Be off by a year or two, and the pros-pects could evaporate or least decline. Anticipate the market — like being a graduate from a top university or college in gas- and oil-related technologies when there's a huge demand — and discover a world of opportunity.

We mention teachers several times in this book because they provide the best, or worst, example of individuals who have thought carefully about their careers and planned their studies, only to have those efforts lead to disappointment. Teachers are not, however, the only group of professionals who have found themselves in this position. In the past, similar things have happened to young adults with degrees in engineering (during the downturn in the oil and gas industry), architecture (when computer-assisted drawing came along), and other targeted and highly specialized fields of study.

As these examples illustrate, there is no way to ensure success. We would, however, recommend that you try to avoid following the crowd. Students who gravitate toward fields that have high demand at the point they leave high school sometimes find that, by the time they have earned a diploma or degree (two to four or more years later), the market conditions have changed. Even more, the majority of high school graduates will likely have headed in that direction, resulting in too many people for the available positions. There is comfort in numbers. Heading where others are going seems, on the surface, to be a safe thing to do. Wrong. Over-production of diploma and degree holders is a key characteristic of the modern training and education system. You really need to find your own way.

> ### TEACHERS: VICTIMS OF CHANGE
>
> Teachers are, in our opinion, the group of professionals who epitomize the reality that, even with careful planning, there are no guarantees that things will work out as planned. These young adults took the courses and did the work they needed to: they completed an undergraduate degree, made it through the highly competitive admission process to teacher education programs, and finished the education degree. But now, the declining number of students has resulted in school closings and — thanks to an over-production of teachers (i.e. teacher training programs graduating more teachers than needed for the changing demographics) — a sharp reduction in available teaching positions. These hard-working, newly minted teachers suddenly find themselves without a job or, in an increasingly common and frustrating situation, with part-time substitute teaching that can last for years. In many instances, the graduates have focused entirely on a teaching career and find themselves unemployed, underemployed, or moving about the country in pursuit of a job.

A great deal rides on the ability of individuals, families, educational institutions, corporations, and governments to bridge the gap between ambition, talent, and need. It's more than sad that so little thought, effort, and honest talk is involved in young adults' decisions about their educational future. Getting a credential can be a wise move or a foolish one. Knowing which it is requires far more thought than most people give to the process.

You may be thinking at this point that we are contradicting ourselves. We keep saying that you need to make careful plans but, at the same time, we tell you that nothing is permanent and guaranteed in the world of work. If the latter is true, what's the point of planning? Why not just get a generalist degree (a three-year BA majoring in nothing in particular) and hope for the best? The answer is that nothing is black and white. Some parts of the labour market are stable: there will always be a demand for doctors, accountants, and some other professionals. (But not, it turns out, for lawyers — that field is overcrowded, facing technological challenges, and coping with out-sourcing.) There will always be jobs for those in the skilled trades, but that's a different point, which we will make later. Jobs may change somewhat, but skills can often be transferrable: if you are great at math, you can use your skills in many fields, some of which may not have developed yet.

But you have to stand out from the crowd. You have to be good at something, but not necessarily a university something. The people in danger are those with low-quality generalist degrees which, however personally fulfilling, may not demonstrate any particular skills and, accordingly, may leave you unemployable in the ever-evolving economy.

PREPARING YOURSELF FOR A CONFUSING WORLD

As a young adult moving into the world beyond high school or looking to improve your current situation, you need to be prepared. Be aware, though, that:

- advice based on the experiences of parents and grandparents does not necessarily apply to current circumstances;

- it is a tough world out there, and the employment situation is going to get more confusing in the near future;

- global forces, corporate structures, and a rapidly changing economy are transforming opportunities for young adults, not always for the better; and,

- opportunities will exist, but they might not match your particular expectations and desires.

The easy way of saying all of this is that it's a rough-and-tumble world and will get more so in the years to come. There is a chance that circumstances will improve dramatically, that jobs will appear when and as wanted by young adults emerging from a self-selected field of study at college or university. And if you believe that, we have some Indonesian gold stocks we want to sell you.[4] There are so many factors at play — from demographics to international economics, from the market demand for university graduates to the fate of the Canadian resource sector — that it is impossible to say with confidence precisely how young Canadians should prepare themselves for adulthood and the world of work.

There is, however, a way forward. It involves careful planning and preparation and a clear and thoughtful assessment of possibilities and options. It requires that you seek out the best possible means of testing and proving yourself, for there is much less space at the top than people currently believe, and tens of thousands of people who want the same opportunities. You need to be careful, methodical, and systematic in your approach. You need to be both realistic about yourself and knowledge-able about how the world of work and employment actually work. Right now — and we say this based on years of working in post-secondary education — far too few young Canadians approach life after high school with the single-mindedness of purpose that is required.

CHAPTER TWO

KNOW YOURSELF

THE IMPORTANCE OF SELF-AWARENESS

There is an underlying myth in contemporary Canadian society that the only way to achieve financial and social success is with at least one university degree. Whether you're a teen about to graduate from high school or a young adult looking to improve your current situation, you undoubtedly have heard endless talk about the importance of going on to university. Studies show that the vast majority of Canadian parents want their children (that's you) to get a degree and to get one of the middle-class careers that you supposedly deserve. When researchers ask high school students what they plan and want to do, the majority say the same thing — go to university. For some of you, this is an ideal choice; for others, it will be a costly and demoralizing mistake — you may hate it, and you may well not succeed.

If we have learned nothing else from our years of experience with our students and with our children, it's this: the best possible decisions in planning for their futures are made by people who take the time to carefully and honestly know themselves. Let's start with the most basic question: how do you know if you are one of the people who would enjoy and benefit from a university education? To give an honest and useful answer, you have to know yourself. You must have a frank conversation with yourself about what you like and dislike, your strengths and weaknesses, your values, and your aspirations. This is not easy, especially for seventeen-year-olds. It's sad but unfortunately true that Canadian society has avoided asking you these questions. Many of you have been told, repeatedly, that you can be anything you want to be — a dangerously misleading piece of advice which, in most cases, is simply not true.

In this chapter, we are going to ask you why, in light in all of the other excellent direct-from-high-school options worth considering, you think that you want to go to university. Getting into a Canadian university is surprisingly simple; getting out with a degree, on the other hand, can be quite difficult. So we'll lead you through a process of self-evaluation designed to show you whether you are ready to go to university and, equally important, whether you are likely to succeed. We want to make sure that you understand the issues, challenges, and possibilities — and that you make good decisions based on a full awareness of your skills, abilities, and motivation. You are likely to find this a bit unnerving, and you might not like what we have to say. Please remember that we have no vested interest in your final decision. But we strongly believe that making informed decisions about your post–high school career will stand you in good stead for the rest of your life.

WISHING DOESN'T MAKE IT SO

Thousands of Canadian high school graduates go to university intending to be medical doctors. They pick their high school courses accordingly and study hard to get high grades. Filled with optimism and dreams of a rewarding medical career and an impressive income, they submit their applications for university, planning to get a degree and then move on to medical school. Of these hopefuls, some drop out of university, while quite a few do not get grades high enough to make applying to medical school worthwhile. One of us served for several years on the admissions panel for a Canadian medical school. The students who made the shortlist (about a quarter to a third of those who applied) were amazing — brilliant marks, volunteer activities that would have overwhelmed Albert Schweitzer, a strong character, and a killer work ethic. Only one in four of the short-listed candidates was accepted; for the rest, the dream of being a doctor turned to disappointment.

DO YOU REALLY WANT TO GO TO UNIVERSITY?

First question, and we ask it again: why are you considering university? Have your parents talked about it for years, and have always assumed that you'd go? Did they make annual contributions to a Registered Education Savings Plan and use this as a regular occasion to remind you of your already-paid-for destiny? Do your teachers and guidance counsellors (if you meet with them) tell you that you are university material? Are your friends all going? Or is it just the background noise of the modern world — from TV shows and movies, from politicians' speeches, newspaper stories, and hallway conversations? Did the university recruiters descend on your high school with tales of an exciting social life, enthusiastic teachers, great programs, excellent career opportunities, and, of course, the highly deceptive statistic that university graduates make $1 million in a career more than college graduates and $1.3 million more than high school graduates?

Regardless of where the pressure comes from — and it comes from all these places and more — the reality is that the importance of going to university is probably hardwired in your brain. At no time in our history have so many Canadian young adults gone to university (over a million undergraduates now, representing roughly a third of all high school graduates), so the decision you are making is a very common one. In Ontario, the largest province, about 130,000 students applied to enter first year of one (or more than one) of the provincial universities in 2012.[1]

Back to the main question: do you really want to go to university? University studies are difficult. If you do attend university, you will be committing yourself to an additional four years of schooling — and that is the minimum, since many students take more time than that. Four or more extra years of being the classroom for eight months of the year with four-month breaks to try to raise enough money to keep going. It is a major commitment of time, money, and effort. Have you really given careful thought to whether or not you are ready for this substantial challenge?

There are some very good reasons for going to university. Note that we do not list among them such socially important things as "because my friends are going," "because I don't know what to do with my life and I need time to think about it," "because I want to make lots of money," or "because my parents want me to go." These actually factor prominently into students' decisions, but have to be considered separately. Your parents may well be right, and you should give careful thought to their ideas and rationale. There will be more about this later.

University is an expensive place to get your head together and, while it works for some young people, most find it difficult to resolve their career and life ambitions while writing essays and cramming for examinations. Your friends, on the other hand, could easily lead you astray. Not many high school friendships — romantic or otherwise — survive the undergraduate years. To put it more gently, they are likely to be replaced by new friendships and partnerships. For now, here are our top four reasons why you should consider going to university, in no particular order of importance:

- **Because you are curious about the world and you love learning.** This is the traditional reason, the one university professors like to think motivates most of their students. Those who approach university from this perspective and who have the requisite skills make the best university students and typically do well after their degree is finished.

- **Because you are academically well prepared and talented, and you wish to test yourself, intellectually and skill-wise, at a higher level.** There is nothing wrong with being competitive and wanting to find out just how good you can be. The greatest benefits from a university education typically go to the best students; if you think you are one of these, then heading to campus can be a fine idea.

- **Because you are truly interested in making the world a better place.** In the 1960s and 1970s, many students who attended university gave up decent job opportunities because they were idealistic and hopeful about creating an improved world. University is a great place to find similar thinkers and to confront the ideas and realities that have shaped the human condition over time.

- **Because you want to pursue a very specific professional career** — engineering, medicine, and the like — and you need a university degree to do so. We have a strong caveat here: a large number of students change their plans mid-degree, based on weaker-than-expected performance or the discovery of new academic and career possibilities. But, if you have a firm sense that you want to try a specific occupational path, university may well be the only way to go.

This list is not long — and it may well be incomplete — but it is a good place to start your self-evaluation. Do you fit into one of these categories? If not, ask yourself the same question we started with: why do you want to go to university? If you do not have a clear and decisive answer to this question, you really would be well advised to give careful thought to alternatives. The happy news, as you will see later, is that there are plenty of good ones. Remember that the number one predictor of young people's likelihood of going to university is whether their parents have university degrees. The second predictor is family income. There is not a lot of "you" in either of these criteria — yet you are the one who is going to have to attend classes, study hard, and complete all of the assignments.

HUMAN CURIOSITY

As you make your plans for going forward, one question hangs over everything else: Are you curious? This seems like an odd question. University, like high school, is a technical and academic challenge. It is supposed to be about study habits, proofreading essays, concentrating on examinations, meeting deadlines, and avoiding long hours at the student pub. And yes, it's about all of those things, and more, but it's much more fundamental — namely, it's about human curiosity.

Well yes, you say, of course I'm curious. Isn't everyone? What we mean by this question, though, is not whether you are curious about Toronto's chances of winning the Stanley Cup in your lifetime (not good) or whether the next version of Starcraft Warrior will be as challenging as the last one (who cares, really), but whether you are curious about intellectual questions — the things of the mind. Do you care about the science and politics of climate change? Feminist interpretations of the writings of Margaret Atwood? The history of Middle Eastern conflicts? The potential of quantum computing? Best practices in Aboriginal self-government? Universities have courses and experts in all of these areas and many others. Look at the course calendar. There are hundreds of faculty members, each with his or her area of interest and expertise. Check them out. This one is an expert on particle physics, that one on Etruscan tomb paintings, the other one on the diseases of fresh-water fish. Do any of them make your intellectual heart beat faster? Do you say "booooooring?" Remember, you will be studying this stuff. Do you really want to? Be honest.

You should be excited about the prospect of venturing into this environment. You should be keen to learn more about subjects you have sampled in high school and intrigued with areas of study that you have never attempted. University is a place tailor-made for intellectual discovery, for chasing down pathways of deep personal interest and for finding academic fields, thinkers, methods, and concepts that you have never even considered.

Many university students — more than in the past, we think, though it's impossible to prove — are not very curious. Influenced by the over-selling of a university education, they march directly from high school to university, having no clear idea why are they are doing so. In this book, we call these students — those who aren't much interested in reading, aren't intellectually curious, and don't engage with what the university has to offer — the *swarm*. They don't find the fact that synchrotron science is unlocking the mysteries of the building blocks of nature very interesting. They are not really keen to learn about the economic foundations of the American Civil War or the religious roots of contemporary terrorism. Very few of them find the nuances of advanced calculus riveting. University professors are deeply — sometimes bizarrely — fascinated by the ins and outs of scholarship, but all too often find themselves staring at students, members of the dreaded swarm, who make no effort to mask their indifference to book learning and to the specifics of a particular course.

IDENTIFYING YOUR INTERESTS

Do you know what interests you? This is more than a scholarly question. We live in an age of mass information — with more informed analysis, factual information, inaccurate data, and partisan commentary available than at any previous time in human history. It dismays us to say so, but a great many students show no interest in any of this information. As a group, university-aged students rarely read newspapers. They dropped reading the paper edition long ago (so did we); but few of them even read the digital editions available on their computers, cellphones, or tablets.

Book sales among young people have dropped precipitously — where would youth publishers be without the Twilight series?

There is a great debate about what has happened to your generation. Don Tapscott, a Canadian digital guru, argues in *Grown Up Digital: How the Net Generation Is Changing Your World* that the Internet age has made young people smarter, more critical, and better with information. You would like him. On the other hand there is Mark Bauerlein, whose wonderfully named book says it all: *The Dumbest Generation: How the Digital Age Stupefies Young Americans and Jeopardizes Our Future (Or, Don't Trust Anyone Under 30)*. He's not your pal. We want Tapscott to be right — and there are sure signs of growing youth confidence. Still, it's not a matter of your intelligence — it's about your approach to learning. You don't need to be Einstein, but you do need to be curious.

The problem is that too large a percentage of the students in most programs and at most universities are not much interested in the world and, therefore, not very inspired by their studies. If you don't follow politics on a regular basis, it's hard to find political science exciting. If you are not genuinely interested in the ordering of the natural world, then biology and geography will simply be abstractions — as bewildering as scientifically illiterate young people find theoretical physics. Ultimately, if you do not enjoy intellectual discovery and enlightenment, then university will be a tedious and completely unsatisfying place.

OUR CURIOSITY TEST

All young people thinking of going to university should give themselves this simple five-point test. It's easy — the easiest of your post-secondary career, with no studying, no pain, and no wrong answers. It is also one of the most important that you will ever take — and we won't be looking over your shoulder. Be honest with yourself (and with your parents who, after all, you are probably counting on to help fund your university studies).

The point of this test is this: if you don't find learning about the physical world, the past and present of humanity, politics, the environment, and the arts interesting when you are in high school, why do you think you would find them interesting in university, which is all about these sorts of things?

CURIOSITY TEST

1. **Do I like to read?** More precisely, have I read many works of serious fiction other than what some teacher has forced me to read as a course requirement in high school? Everyone who graduates from high school can read and write, more or less, but many have not read anything serious beyond course requirements. By "serious," we mean nothing with zombies in it or crazy nonsense about the Catholic Church (we're looking at you, Dan Brown), and at least something about the human condition past Oprah's self-help books.

2. **Do I read high quality non-fiction?** Not a biography of the boys of One Direction, but at least Malcolm Gladwell if not Andrew Nikiforuk or Naomi Klein or Jeff Rubin or Linda McQuaig. Do I read the newspaper or major magazines (*Maclean's*, *Harpers*, *The Walrus*) on a regular basis? It is okay to include the online versions of these publications or even exclusively online news sources, like the *Huffington Post*.

3. **Do I watch foreign films,** art films, CBC documentaries, or thoughtful PBS programs or series? If I watch horror films or films starring Adam Sandler, that doesn't make me a bad person (well, perhaps Sandler is going a bit too far). No one can deal with important and serious stuff all the time. But if I watch reality TV regularly and have never watched a PBS program or a film in a language other than English, then my answer to this question will be "no."

4. **Am I troubled or excited about world affairs?** Tensions in the Middle East, American presidential elections, developments in stem cell technologies, or the economic rise of China. When

a question arises about some aspect of these issues, do I seek out specific information online or in the library? Does it bother me when I know next to nothing about a country, personality, issue, or debate that has burst into prominence? When I heard about the bombing in Boston, did I know where Chechnya was? If not, did I look it up?

5. **Do I enjoy learning?** Do I go to museums and art galleries, go to public lectures, listen to readings at the library, and otherwise engage with the world of ideas? Would I go to listen to a speech by David Suzuki or Stephen Harper (you don't have to like either of them) or Elizabeth May? Do I know who Elizabeth May is? Am I interested in the physical world — astronomy, the exploration of space, the Higgs boson, the evolution of species? Do I watch *Nova* on the American Public Broadcasting System?

So, how did you do? If you answered yes to most, if not all, of these, there is an above-average chance that you will enjoy university and do well. Curious students succeed in university, assuming that their basic skills (writing, reading, and math) are up to university standards and that they avoid the social pitfalls of university life.

Curiosity is the rocket fuel of the academy. If you arrive with the tank fully topped up, you will likely find the experience exciting, demanding, and eye-opening. You will be one of the students who ask spontaneous questions in class, come to a professor's office with questions before the assignment is due (and not just to ask for an extension), attend extra-curricular lectures, and have trouble picking courses because there are too many interesting things to study. We love having you in class. You make universities dynamic and exciting places.

We know that many of you will have looked at the questions and wondered why they are relevant. They actually tell us almost everything we need to know about you. If you answered them all in the negative but still have great high school grades, you can probably survive university, but it may seem like a four-year stint in a dentist's chair — unless someone lights an intellectual fire under you. You will be clever but disengaged; not a happy state in a university.

If you answered negatively but have average grades (80 percent or less in most provinces), then you might be able to complete university — maybe — but your experience will be a tough slog. You will probably struggle with basic assignments and will have trouble figuring out all the fuss about the university experience. If you answered negatively and have poor grades (anything under 75 percent, a figure we will discuss later), you probably should not be in university. The combination of limited interest in the world and poor basic skills puts you at risk from the beginning. Find something else to do, because your university time (likely to be limited to one or two painful years) will be boring, unsatisfying, and a waste of everyone's time.

If you are in the final group, by the way, do not feel bad. About one-third of university students are in this category, and they often leave without a degree. It doesn't mean that they are bad people, nor that they are necessarily unintelligent. It just means that they, like you, are not interested in what university has to offer, and don't have the skills to compensate for this lack of interest. They like other things, and they will be happier and probably more prosperous doing what they like rather than what parents and society think they ought to do. They should instead do what they love and what they are good at, with a firm eye on finding something that will provide a decent income.

Think of it this way. A person who doesn't like music or is not interested in how it is composed and performed is not likely to attend music school. Someone who hates competitive athletics does not go to a month-long sports camp. People who find politics boring and unimportant rarely volunteer for election campaigns. Sending an uncurious young person to university is cruel and wrong, for the student and for the institution. University professors may try to inspire these students, but that's like casting seed on stony ground, and it will not produce many flowers. Test yourself. If you cannot pass the curiosity test, university is probably not for you — or at least it won't be a pleasant experience for you.

SUCCESS: PERSONAL QUALITIES THAT MAKE A DIFFERENCE

There are many ways to succeed in life, depending on how you define success. A rich family or a large inheritance can help — and family income and social position still constitute the single most important determinant of financial well-being in Canada. But this country has considerable mobility, both upward and downward. No one is guaranteed success in life, nor are young people necessarily defined by family circumstances. Canadians have more social mobility — and remember that this means both up and down the social and financial scale — than people in the United States, long celebrated as the land of opportunity. So don't be discouraged if you don't come from a rich family. Many of this country's wealthiest and most powerful people came from families of modest means, working their way up the social, financial, and career ladders.

What personal qualities, then, are most likely to produce the kind of future that young adults want? Unfortunately, luck has a lot to do with it. Being in the right place at the right time, getting a unique job opportunity, buying the right stock or piece of real estate, or making a random choice that works out well are probably as important as some of the more classic characteristics in determining life prospects. But smart people capitalize on luck and do not turn their backs on chances. Thousands of people had the opportunity to purchase ocean-front property in British Columbia in the 1970s, when a few thousand dollars would have been enough to get a nice view lot. Not many people leaped at the chance. Those who did were likely to see their purchases turn into half a million dollars in a couple of decades, finding themselves set for life by a fairly simple — and, in retrospect obvious — decision made thirty years ago. The same is true of buying Apple or Microsoft stock.

Researchers have been trying for years to unlock the secret to human success, without a great deal of consensus on the matter. For decades, people were focused on IQ (Intelligence Quotient), believing, reasonably it seemed, that smart people would do better in life than not-so-smart people. That turns out not to be entirely the case. There are a lot of very smart, high-IQ people, often with impressive academic records, who have had quite average lives in terms of income and career opportunities. Philosophy professors are usually highly intelligent, but they don't make millions — though at least they can be philosophical about it. Analysts also consider a new quantitative measure, Emotional Intelligence (EQ), which determines people's ability to understand, control, and direct their emotions. In our child-obsessed world, the emphasis on IQ and EQ proved very attractive to parents, who directed their children toward expensive IQ- and EQ-enhancing experiences (Mozart music in the crib, and so on), believing that they could, in the process, produce better career and life outcomes for their boys and girls.

We will leave the debate on fundamental brain or intellectual characteristics that determine personal success to the next generation or two of psychologists and neuro-scientists. This does not, however, mean that we do not have strong ideas about the personal qualities that separate those who will succeed in life from those who will struggle (absent great luck or a wealthy family) to get ahead. Paul Tough's insightful book *How Children Succeed* is important in understanding the conditions that produce young people likely to have solid skills and the abilities necessary to make the most of their circumstances. In the sombre opening to his book, Tough documents how early-life trauma — in the form of violence, conflict, severe crisis, or poverty — can stifle individual potential, to the point where recovery is extremely difficult. If anyone ever needs a motivation for early childhood interventions (birth to kindergarten), *How Children Succeed* provides it in spades. If you have made it to the point of high school graduation, there is a strong likelihood that you did not experience early childhood trauma or, if you did, you have one of the other qualities that underlie individual opportunity.

Paul Tough argues that there are three characteristics that determine the chances an individual has to succeed:

- **Grit:** The path through life is littered with trials, crises, and failures. There is nothing about life in the modern world that is easy, obvious, or automatic. Successful people possess real grit — the ability to push through obstacles, respond to challenges, and dust themselves off even after major failures. The drive to succeed is strong in such individuals. They typically take a major set-back as a learning opportunity rather than as a sign of fundamental weakness or shortcoming. Hardship provides important learning opportunities. Demonstrating the ability to work through crises is one of the most important illustrations of a person's capacity for personal growth, adaptation, and simple drive.

- **Curiosity:** Successful people are curious about pretty much everything. They tend to read a great deal and are constantly learning. They love to explore, experiment, discover, and understand. Teachers know the difference between someone who truly wants to learn and one who studies for a good grade. The former are treasures; the latter tend to whine a lot. The will to learn and the desire to discover sit at the core of all truly successful people.

- **Character:** Much as schools and society at large would like to reduce the requirements for success to a series of teachable moments or easily transmitted characteristics, there is, according to Tough, a great deal more at play. Personal qualities (that is, character) matter a great deal — trumping IQ and many other characteristics in determining the likelihood of success. A person of strong character has easily observable and highly desirable qualities: the ability to respond to adversity; real and sustained persistence; life focus, reliability, and trustworthiness; and an overwhelming work ethic. People with good character do not blame others for their shortcomings; instead, they grasp opportunities to learn and develop, and do not let life's misfortunes deter them from their long-term goals.

It's important to note that self-esteem is missing from Tough's description. For the past generation, schools and parents have been preoccupied with ensuring that children feel good about themselves — even if this means moving away from competition (too much losing), not holding children responsible for meeting standards (too much reliance on arbitrary educational goals), and not drawing attention to differences in performance and ability (creating divisions within social groups). Self-esteem, it turns out, is not well connected to academic performance or career outcomes.

A PERSONAL SWOT ANALYSIS

Here, perhaps, is the hardest bit. You are graduating from high school with decent grades. Your grades probably average over 80 percent — you are an A student! Alas, this is not nearly the achievement that it was two generations ago. In 1960, fewer than 5 percent of all university applicants had grades that high. Now, over two-thirds of all young adults attending university do. The reason for this is mostly grade inflation in the high schools. If you are right at 80 you are just below the average among students considering university — hardly a sign of a world-beater! You want to make the right choice, and you are considering your options.

We have already given you a series of tests that should give you a bit of a sense about how you might fit at university. Here's another one:

Given that professional economists, demographers, and others have serious difficulties anticipating market and social trends, do not be surprised if you find forecasting the next year, let alone the next decade, to be extremely hard. The baby boomers are holding on to their jobs, sometimes because they are paying for their children's education! Restructuring inside companies and governments has eliminated thousands of middle-class jobs, just as closing manufacturing plants has removed thousands more (and unions, eager to protect existing workers, have increasingly turned to two-tier contracts to protect benefits for the older employees at the cost of new workers). Underemployment — getting a job that requires far fewer skills and less education than an individual has — has become widespread. In the United States, 25 percent of all retail workers have university degrees, as do 15 percent of all taxi drivers[2] and 15 percent of all firefighters.[3]

FOLLOWING YOUR DREAM ...

A friend's daughter had tons of academic and professional skills — but she really loved to cook. She cooked when she was a pre-teen, when she babysat, and all through high school. It finally dawned on her that she really, really wanted to cook. So she went to cooking school, got a diploma, and now, in high demand as a pastry chef, makes a decent living doing precisely what she loves to do.

The most important part of this story is that her parents let her follow her passion and did not, as so many parents do these days, insist on her pursuing a more standard academic path.

SWOT TEST

1. **What are your strengths?** As with the other questions in this test, compiling a list — in this case of your strengths — can be difficult. You have to be brutally honest. A strength might not simply be the courses where you had the highest grades (you might have had an easy marker for a teacher), but rather a field that you enjoyed and had decent grades in.

2. **What are your weaknesses?** Weaknesses require introspection. How hard do you work? Are you really prepared to make major sacrifices in order to get ahead?

3. **What opportunities are available to support your success?** The real challenges rest with identifying opportunities and threats. When it comes to opportunities, most students rely on parents, teachers, government, and the general "buzz" about the economy and about career possibilities. This advice is notoriously unreliable, offered by people who will not be living your life. There are opportunities in emerging fields, like nanotechnology. And, of course, there always will be jobs in the service and retail sectors.

4. **What threats could thwart your plans for success?** There are threats from Chinese and South Asian manufacturers and competition from professionals in India. There will be jobs in the western Canadian resource sector, but many fewer if pipelines and transportation links to markets are not developed.

Why? First, there are so many applicants with higher-education credentials that university graduates are getting jobs that used to go to high school graduates. Second, there are so many more people with undergraduate degrees than there are jobs that require degrees that many have to take work that does not require a degree — notably in the retail sector.[4] Many university graduates are working alongside young adults who did not go to university at all, have four more years of experience and earnings, and, in many cases, higher pay and several steps forward on the promotion ladder.

This situation should all be part of your SWOT analysis. Determining where you will fit in a rapidly evolving society and economy is no mean feat. We will come back to this over and over again: there is no substitute for real excellence — the top opportunities typically go to the very best — and hard work and good character will carry you much further than a basic credential any day. The top students in every field — including ones that seem devoid of career opportunities — will find meaningful and interesting work, although not without some difficulty.

BEYOND SWOT: KNOWING WHERE YOU STAND

This leads to another series of questions that you have to ask about yourself as you make your plans for the next and crucial stage in your life:

- **How good are you at academics?** Forget your grades. Do a realistic assessment of your classmates. Are you the top student in the school? In the top ten? Here is your first wake-up call. There are hundreds of high schools in Ontario. New Brunswick has dozens of them. Each of these has a graduating class. Assume you are one of the top ten students in your school. This means that there are thousands of students in the country's high schools of the same calibre and general ability as you. Are you ready to compete with the very best?

- **How hard do you work?** This is not a question just about academics. It relates to how you do your homework, to be sure, but also how you do with household chores, volunteer activities, and your part-time job. Do you tackle assignments — regardless of the nature of the work — with enthusiasm and efficiency? Or do you take your time or complain about what you have been asked to do? Which kind of person, by the way, would you hire if you were doing the hiring?

- **What do you do really well?** Think about your real interests in life. Make a list of the areas where you excel. These can be academic, physical, musical, artistic, or practical. Note if you are great at physics or English, but also if you are top-notch at carpentry or art. Give a lot of thought to this list, for it is going to be extremely important in defining your post–high school options. If, for example, you are not good at mathematics and you got your grades up to a competitive level only by taking the same course three times, you probably should not pursue a math-based college or university program. If, on the other hand, you are naturally gifted at mechanical or technical work to the exclusion of other more traditional academic skills, surely this should factor into your decision-making.

- **What do you do badly?** Make a second list — and be really honest with yourself here — about the kind of things that you do badly. For the purposes of this exercise, define "badly" as being those things where you are in the bottom half of your peer group. If half of your high school classmates do something significantly better than you, whether it is writing, understanding world affairs, working with computers, grasping science, or fixing a bicycle or car, then you need to put this down. In some instances, these areas of weakness can be overcome. If you really want to pursue work in a field related to computers and you have minimal skills, challenge yourself. Take extra courses, outside of high school if necessary, to upgrade. A weakness need not be permanent, but a key weakness unaddressed can cause real difficulties down the road.

- **What do you really love doing?** This is where the difficulty starts, particularly if your parents have different ambitions for you. Many parents have dreams of their children becoming a doctor, lawyer, accountant, or engineer. Very few, it seems, fantasize about their children working at a day-care centre, working in a pulp mill, getting a clerk's job in a provincial government office, or becoming a carpenter's apprentice. Dealing with your parents' hopes for your future can be a real problem — and it often starts here. You need to make a clear list about the things you really and truly love to do. What gets you excited in terms of study, work, and recreation? What kinds of activities make a real difference to your life and bring you simple and unadulterated joy? How much does money matter to you? You need to be completely honest with yourself and with your parents about this one. There are great jobs out there — social worker, musician, youth counsellor, minister, pre-school teacher, gardener — that offer full and fulfilling lives. But the pay is low, and working conditions often can be very difficult. If money is a prime motivating factor in your life, then you had best take this into account. Many jobs simply will not provide the $100,000 a year salary, suburban house, holidays in the Caribbean, and two cars in the garage that many of you aspire to. If you want to earn a lot of money, there are ways of doing so: entrepreneurship (high risk, high potential return), medicine, accounting, some parts of the law, or real estate speculation. There are even a few places — out west and in the North for the most part — where it is possible to combine high wages and low skills. See what heavy-duty mechanics make at the diamond mine at Ekati — you will be impressed — and they generally have not gone to university or, if they have, they don't use their training on the job. If money is the object, you had better have a prodigious work ethic, have a specialized skill, or be willing to follow the cash across the country.

- **How much do you know about the world of work?** You are facing one of the most important decisions in your life — preparing your-self for the workforce — when you know, typically, very little about career options. We know that high schools offer courses in career planning, but — based on the experiences of our children — we sense that most teenagers don't take them very seriously. This is a serious question. There are thousands of careers available, from cat skinner (not what you think) to archivist. You could be a genetics counsellor or a nanotechnologist. There is a large need for power engineers and millwrights, occupational therapists, glaziers, epide-miologists, diagnostic medical sonographers, speech pathologists, cost estimators, audit clerks, and a great many more.

- **Are you willing to relocate for work?** In your grandparents' days, there was no question — they would move to wherever there was a job. Canadians used to move a great deal, following their dreams and job opportunities across the country and even around the world. This is still true for many Canadians, which is why there are so many Newfoundlanders in Fort McMurray these days. It turns out, however, that many of you are not very mobile. Torontonians have trouble imagining life outside the city. (Trust us, it can be great.) Young adults from Vancouver and Victoria (a.k.a. paradise) are notorious for refusing to leave. Highly motivated young people in the Maritimes have historically been willing, even eager, to relocate to other parts of the country, but others have trouble leaving St. John's, Saint John, Charlottetown, or Halifax. Ask yourself this question: Would you, Toronto person, once you finish your schooling, happily relocate to Fort McMurray, a dynamic city at the heart of the oil sands? Would you consider a job in an isolated Aboriginal community, where there is often an urgent need for professionals? Would you consider Saskatchewan — yes, it is cold, but any place that is home to the Roughriders is pretty neat — where the economy is booming? How about Whitehorse in the Yukon or Yellowknife in the Northwest Territories, two of the most fascinating communities in the country? Mobility has always been the great equalizer in Canada, creating career and life opportunities for individuals. Look deep inside yourself. Will you move to opportunity or do you expect opportunity to find you? (Subtle hint here: Mobility is one of the greatest keys to full career development, while staying put can lock you in a career and income box for life, even if it makes your mother happy.) Spread your wings: you might like the place, and you don't have to live there forever.

- **Are you willing to create your own job?** We will come back to this point later, but entrepreneurship and self-employment are critical components of the modern economy. We have many self-employed people — taxi drivers in some cities, convenience-store owners, tax specialists and the like — but far too few entrepreneurs — the people who create companies, products, services, and jobs. Do you really want to work for someone else, or are you willing to set out on your own? Self-employment is growing rapidly — along with all of its freedoms and risks. Where do you fit in the spectrum from risk taking to excessive caution?

PEER PRESSURE: RESISTING THE SWARM

One of the greatest challenges facing young adults is breaking away from the group. Much as everyone likes to believe that he or she is an original, a true individual, the reality is that we are shaped and defined by our genetics, environment, and social relations. Students from schools in wealthy areas are more likely to go to university than are those from poor districts. If you hang around with the swarm, your chances of doing well in high school decline and your post-secondary prospects get dimmer. We are conditioned by popular culture, peer attitudes, and a desire to fit in. This is simply the truth.

Ironically, one of the most significant outcomes of contemporary peer pressure has been the routine migration from high school to university. Everyone — from parents to friends — talks incessantly about university. In the best public schools, "where are you applying?" and "where are you going?" are the main questions. At elite American private secondary schools — which often advertise the success of their graduates in terms of numbers being accepted with scholarships into the best universities — the pressure to write the SAT (Scholastic Aptitude Test, required for admission to most U.S. colleges and universities) and prepare dynamite application letters is intense.

There is a certain lemming-like character to this movement toward universities, for it is simply assumed that all right-minded young people will move from high school to campus, joining the mass competition to get a cubicle job (read *Dilbert* if you don't already do so: it's a fascinating and hilarious window on the world you have been trained for) and an entry ticket to the middle class. There is not a lot of "U" in university but rather a great deal of "US," as in "we are all going to university." Politicians have picked up on this, of course, which is why they talk about university so much — and why Dalton McGuinty, former premier of Ontario, federal

Liberal leader Justin Trudeau, and U.S. President Barack Obama have hinted that every young person should have the chance to go, or should *actually* go (they were vague about which it should be) to university.

Overcoming peer pressure is not easy. We appreciate that. University recruiters learned many years ago that one of the best ways of increasing applications from a specific high school was to convince a handful of popular kids to attend their institution. Once they had locked in these leaders — the captain of the basketball team and the head cheerleader were, stereotypically, the targets — many others followed more or less automatically. There will be a very strong desire to follow your friends, both in the decision to attend university and then in the collective choice of campus, typically the one closest to your high school. Everything is familiar then, isn't it? You can take your social circle with you, stay in familiar territory, probably live at home. All very comfy — but not a very adventurous leap into adulthood.

BE YOURSELF

Our advice, avuncular as always, is simple: be yourself; and, if you don't know who you are, find out. When the swarm forms up, make your own judgments about whether or not you want to join. Stand aside, look far afield, re-evaluate your SWOT analysis, and contemplate your future — for yourself and by yourself. Live your own life — not the one that your friends have outlined for you. It's easier to give this advice than to follow it, but the results will justify the effort.

CHAPTER THREE

THE UNIVERSITY OPTION

TAKE THE TIME TO DO IT RIGHT

Many of you who are giving serious attention to your future will opt for university. Some of you will have made the right decision — for you, university is a great choice, and you are perhaps wondering why we are fussing about it so much. Your path is clear and, barring some misfortune, your success is assured.

For others, though, the decision is wrong. You will be disappointed with university and, in a year or so, you may wish that you had listened to our warnings. You need to focus on planning, and going to university without thinking about what you are doing — treating it as an extension of high school, living at home, and following the high school swarm to the local campus — is not planning. This too-common approach is one of the reasons so many students struggle and fail in their first year. You can make the choice that's best for you and, if you decide on university, there are things you can do to prepare yourself for it — take the time to do it right.

INVEST TIME IN YOUR PLANNING

Going to university is a very big decision — one that can cost you and your family $30,000 or much more, depending on how long it takes you to finish your diploma or degree, and what costs you factor in (more later on costs). Some of your parents have money socked away for you, thanks to the Canadian tax system with its rewards for upper-middle-class people sending their children to university. However, many of you will have to rely

SHAD VALLEY

Canada has a superb testing ground for students who want to find out more about their potential and their ability. Shad Valley is a highly competitive national program for elite high school students, designed to challenge them intellectually and to help them identify potential areas of study and work. Students, almost 600 of them in 2013, gather on select campuses across Canada for boot-camp-like month-long sessions, provided by the best teachers at the university. The academic sessions are wonderful, the other students excellent, and the instructors and coordinators are among the most inspirational and demanding that you can find anywhere.

If you are in grade ten, eleven, or twelve and think of yourself as bright, talented, curious, creative, motivated, and determined, move heaven and earth to get into a Shad Valley session. You will likely meet Canada's future leaders, have a terrific time, and learn a great deal about yourself. Shad Valley also offers the best possible introduction to the excitement of the university system. If you cannot be inspired by the promise and the reality of Shad Valley, then the chance of your being an outstanding student at university or a top-notch professional thereafter are pretty small. It's such an elite option, though, and you have to be so good to become one of the 600, that anyone who is motivated and eligible to participate is probably going to be a winner at university anyway.

There are many ways that you can try to separate yourself from the crowd. Shad Valley is, in our estimation, probably the best.

on some combination of savings from work, loans (private or government), family support, grants, and scholarships. It's a long and quite expensive haul. Doing it right is important. Don't be distracted by the agonies of high school graduates in the United States — desperate to get into the prestigious university of their choice, where only the best apply to Harvard, which turns down more than 90 percent of them. No Canadian university rejects anywhere near that percentage of applicants, and some accept almost anyone who applies. Relax — you will always get in somewhere. The question is whether you really want to, and whether you should.

One of the problems we have in Canada is that it is too easy to make the decision to apply to university, and too easy to get in. Our academic standards, save for a handful of elite programs in elite universities, are not very high. Almost everyone with a high school average over 75 percent as a high school average and the right mix of courses will be able to find a place at one of the country's universities. We now have decent university campuses not only in major cities but also in almost every town of substantial size in the country — from Corner Brook, Newfoundland, to Orillia, Ontario, and on to Prince George, British Columbia — so you probably do not need to look very far from home. Because the local campuses are so accessible, both physically and academically, you, like most Canadian students, may simply opt for the university closest to you.

It's also easy to apply to university. Ontario and British Columbia have common application systems. Fill out one form, pay the fees, and the government will send your high school grades directly to the institutions you have selected. Some permit you to submit supplementary material — an explanation for why grades of 65 percent do not really represent your inner genius or a description of the extra-curricular activities that make you a natural leader, suitable for admission to the country's best undergraduate programs. Then you sit back and wait. Nothing to it! Most students do not even visit the campuses that they have applied to. Reputations are pretty much fixed in Canada: students, counsellors, and parents are much more likely to push Queen's, Western Ontario (now, for some silly branding reason, Western University), or Alberta than they are to select St. Thomas, Brandon, or Lakehead — even though each of these schools is a better choice for many students.

This, unfortunately, is where many students make a major mistake. Picking the right university is a difficult task that should be taken seriously. There are many factors to take into account. Universities pretend publicly that they are all the same, all great teaching and research institutions, but it isn't true, and students react differently to them. Some students love the place where they earn their degree, while others forget about it and its faculty as soon as the degree is conferred. It's important to realize that not every university will suit you.

THE AMERICAN DREAM

The American model is influential in this country. In the United States, a combination of media hype about the very top schools (Harvard, Stanford, Duke, Yale, Princeton, and the like) and representations in popular culture of campus life (*Animal House, Legally Blonde, Good Will Hunting, Accepted, Old School* or, more recently, *The Social Network* and *Admissions*), along with college sports (particularly football and basketball), generates endless conversations about college selection.

Indeed, probably more Canadian students fantasize about attending an Ivy League school or getting into UCLA than dream about an acceptance letter from the University of Calgary or Laurentian.

PLAN TO VISIT SEVERAL CAMPUSES

For most high school students, universities can be imposing and even intimidating places. Since you may be spending four or more years at the place, there is a lot to gain from a campus visit, even if you avoid one of the promotional university tours and simply wander about with friends and family or on your own. A quick look at one of the huge classrooms — several at the biggest universities hold over a thousand students — can be a real shock. The athletically minded should check out the sports facilities. Some campuses have superb gyms, pools, rinks, and fitness centres. As a legacy of the 1988 Winter Olympics, the University of Calgary has some of the best athletic facilities anywhere.

You should take a good look at the residences too, particularly since we strongly urge you to stay in residence. They vary widely in quality: some are pretty spiffy; others are old and shabby. Pay close attention to student spaces — cafeterias, study rooms, lounges, and social rooms. You will be surprised by the difference between most of the Ontario universities — which have been starved of building funds for years — and the more prosperous institutions in Saskatchewan, Alberta, and British Columbia. Heritage buildings add immensely to the ambiance of campus life. The University of Saskatchewan and Toronto's University College are excellent in this category, to say nothing of the old buildings at McGill. But not all of the impressive buildings are old. Find the Irving Building at Acadia University or the "Ike" Barber Library at UBC if you want to see what generous donations can produce for Canadian universities.

Eating is a big part of the campus experience, and universities work hard to collect your food money. We are not fans of food courts, which typically feature chain restaurants, but there are great cafeteria facilities at many universities. When your parents aren't looking, check out the student pubs, especially for signs announcing music, comedy, and events other than just boozing. All work and no play and all that.

As physical places, the universities range widely, from barren suburban campuses like York University (architecturally a one-star place) to lovely settings like Acadia University in Nova Scotia. Urban universities often sprawl over many city blocks, while the park-like campuses at Queen's, University of Saskatchewan, and Western Ontario occupy many hectares. Their sheer size can be fairly intimidating. Wander onto the Orwellian[1] mountaintop campus of Simon Fraser University — not our favourite place, architecturally speaking, though it was designed by the famous Arthur Erickson. Some of the best universities — the University of Toronto and Université de Quebéc à Montréal spring to mind — are visually unimpressive, with major roads dividing the campus and hodge-podge buildings. U of T is known for its beautiful 19th-century residences and lecture halls, but these share space with the concrete monstrosities that passed for urban design in the 1960s and 1970s — not for nothing is its Robarts Library (1973) nicknamed "Fort Book."

The setting for the University of British Columbia is so stunning that some students undoubtedly decide to attend simply to enjoy what is one of the nicest university settings in the world. (There's a nude beach just off campus too, for those who are interested.) The University of Northern British Columbia (UNBC) is the best-designed campus in Canada — we say as homers, having both worked there, Bill for nearly twenty years — and the attractiveness of the campus really adds to student life. Vancouver Island University in Nanaimo has the loveliest view of any university in Canada, though the buildings are less appealing. Look up the two satellite campuses of the University of Waterloo — the architecture school in Cambridge and the digital media campus in Stratford — if you want two excellent examples of how first-rate design can have a profound and positive impact on campus life. Conversely, a walk around academically impressive Dalhousie University is more than a little depressing, just as the research-intensive University of Alberta is hard to love in an aesthetic way. You are going to spend a lot of time on campus — make sure that the place feels good for you.

From the perspective of their physical space, all universities accomplish their core functions in pretty much the same way. All the universities have libraries, lecture halls, faculty and administrative offices, sports facilities, and the like. Some look like large high schools; others like small cities. Some have invited commerce right onto campus (in the form of fast-food joints and stores); others are as sterile as a Stalinist government office. After the first blush of excitement — or dismay — whichever university you choose simply becomes your home.

CHECK EVERYTHING OUT

Your campus visit should be much more comprehensive than a simple tour of the buildings and grounds. It is vital that you find the other services and supports that the university has to offer. Find out about the special programs for first-year students — you need to know what the institution does to help students adjust to the campus. Make sure you locate the writing, math, and study skills centres at the university. While you may think you won't need such support, the chances are better than even that you will. When you need help, you'll need it in a hurry. And, since your university career may depend on them, you need the services to be first-rate. There are other things worth checking out: counselling, career advising, co-operative education, health services, and financial assistance. And don't forget the people in the registrar's office. They're the ones who handle all of your administrative work, process your grades, and otherwise monitor your progress through your years of study. Treat them with respect; they're not your servants, and they can be helpful in times of stress.

Some of the stuff you hear on a campus visit won't be of much importance to you. Guides will tell you about famous alumni, social life, guest lectures, great facilities, major donations to enrich university life, and a great deal of other good news. You need to look more deeply. Try to get a sense of the people on campus. See if you can meet with some faculty members, departmental advisers (the people who guide you through your academic program), and, in particular, the staff. It will surprise you to learn that support staff — departmental secretaries, janitors, cafeteria workers, residence advisers, reference librarians — can have a great influence on your enjoyment of campus life.

SAMPLE ACCEPTANCE RATES

Canadian universities:

Queen's	40%
Western	58%
Manitoba	67%
Cape Breton	88%
Waterloo	20 to 58%*

International universities:

Hong Kong	9%
Duke	11%
Cal State Northridge†	74%
Harvard	6%
Tokyo	20%
Cambridge (U.K.)	22%
Indian Institutes of Technology	2%

*depending on program
†a non-elite US institution

You need to find the campus that suits you, and you alone — not your friends, not your parents, and certainly not your high school teachers or advisers. Academic matters are, in the end, more important than the football stadium. Finding the right degree is much more crucial than having a climbing wall in the gymnasium, a fancy buffeteria, or lap swimming in the university pool. But the people do matter a great deal. Look at the campus carefully — and find the university that fits best with your personality, aspirations, and academic needs.

DON'T BE TOO IMPRESSED THAT YOU GOT IN

Your mother's tears of joy when you open the letter of acceptance from (fill in the name of your university) are a tad over the top. It's not hard to get into a Canadian university, including some of the very best in the country. Canada has many university spaces that it needs to fill every year. While every institution would love to fill up with straight-A students who carry 92 percent averages, high-level athletic and musical ability, and tons of community service, the reality is that they need to pay the bills. So, each year, each university reviews its cut-off point (the lowest grade average for entry), typically on a faculty-by-faculty basis. If there are lots of applications, the cut-off rate goes up. If the application pool dries up — as happens quite often in western Canada when there is a shortage of workers (people choose high oil patch wages over a university education) — the institution will lower the cut-off point. For several reasons it's harder to get into the University of Toronto than Brandon, but elite international institutions have a much higher bar than even the best Canadian universities.

Canadians are proud of the fact that this country values accessibility over elitism. But elitism, in the context of universities, means simply that the students on average are smart, or able, or intelligent, whichever word you like. In the United States, elite also means that the university is unusually expensive; in Canada, all universities outside Quebec are fairly equally priced. The fact is that really smart students do better at university and have much higher success rates. The less smart ones have a high dropout rate. The easier it is to get in — the lower the standards, to put it bluntly — the smaller the percentage of students who graduate and, often, the less engaging the classes will be.

Statistics Canada says that the first-year dropout rate at thirteen Canadian universities is 30 percent,[2] but it differs widely from place to place.[3] Getting into a top university and a high-demand academic program is an impressive accomplishment. Acceptance by an institution that accepts almost everyone is like being able to get into a new movie at the local theatre. Show up at the right time, pay the entrance fee, and you are in. Not a major achievement. So, celebrate if you got into the university of your choice, but realize that this is no guarantee of success.

PICK THE CAMPUS, NOT THE CITY

Two of the strongest influences on university choice are contradictory: the desire to stay home with family and friends and the desire to take the fast track out of town. This is hardly surprising. Seventeen- and eighteen-year-olds respond to the challenges of growing up and their changing relationship with their parents in different ways. It's not unusual to have one sibling eager to flee the family home and another clinging to his bedroom. (The same holds for parents. Some want the teenagers out of the house and away from town, while others, determined to postpone the empty nest syndrome, dread the idea of their children moving away.) We hope that you will think carefully about your motivations for going to university — and for picking a campus either a longish bus ride away or moving across the country.

In the United States, there are many colleges and universities in towns of under 20,000 people — often called simply college towns. This is not the Canadian pattern. Canada's biggest and arguably best universities are in the major cities (UBC, Calgary, Alberta, Manitoba, Toronto, Ottawa, McGill, Laval) or large centres (Saskatchewan, Western Ontario, Victoria, Dalhousie,

---

GET OUT OF TORONTO

If you are from the Greater Toronto Area, unless you are interested in a program that you can get only at the U of T, York, or Ryerson, go to university somewhere else, preferably as far away as possible.

Do you want to be one of those Toronto people who has never lived anywhere else in Canada, whose interests are limited by the Leafs, the subway system, and the *Toronto Star*? We hope you are a broader person than that. The same holds true for Vancouverites: get out of Lotus Land and experience your country.

Queen's). There are no universities with more than 15,000 students in cities of under 50,000 people. Compared to the United States, Canada has only a small number of universities in old-fashioned college towns where the students make up a significant part of the population: Bishop's (Lennoxville, Quebec), Mount Allison (Sackville, New Brunswick), St. Francis Xavier (Antigonish, Nova Scotia), Acadia (Wolfville, Nova Scotia). Most of the so-called small-town universities in Canada are in sizeable cities such as Peterborough (120,000 people), Sudbury (160,000), Brandon (56,000), and Prince George (71,000).

Many students, particularly from smaller towns and rural areas, are attracted by the lure of the big city, coupled with the chance to get away from home. Size is not the only determinant. While large, sophisticated Montreal is a student favourite, Halifax is also a major attraction, much more so than larger cities such as Calgary or Hamilton. Sudbury (Laurentian), Sault St. Marie (Algoma), Prince George (UNBC), and other blue-collar towns are not drawing cards for their universities. While we understand the appeal, of both small towns and big cities, we urge you to emphasize the campus rather than the surrounding community. Pick Simon Fraser University, not Vancouver. Don't be deterred by the size of Wolfville (which is a lovely town anyway) but rather focus on the appeal of Acadia, one of the country's most attractive institutions. For the right student, Brandon is an ideal fit, while for others the University of Winnipeg is the perfect place. You study on the campus, not in the town or city. Don't make it a major criterion for your university choice.

THINK SMALL (UNIVERSITY)

The international reputation of a university is set by its faculty members and graduate programs, save for the American premium liberal arts and science colleges. As an entering university student, you need not be overly impressed by sky-high research rankings and the sterling reputations of leading faculty members. In fact, star academics only rarely teach undergraduate courses, so don't be too excited about being on the same campus as a Nobel Prize winner. Focus instead on the quality of the undergraduate experience. In one of the best books written on American colleges, *Colleges That Change Lives*, author Loren Pope argued that the best educational opportunities in the United States were to be found in small, specialized colleges, not in the big-name universities.

The same is true, to a degree, in Canada, even though we do not have a deep tradition of small liberal arts colleges. There are no Canadian equivalents of Swarthmore, Middlebury, Harvey Mudd College, Lewis and Clark, Colorado College, and Reed. There is one attempt underway, at Quest University in Squamish, British Columbia, to import the model of the high-quality, high-cost private university into Canada, but it remains experimental at this early stage in its history.

The biggest universities — Toronto, UBC, Alberta, Ottawa, York — typically cram first-year students into large lecture classes, often taught by graduate students and part-time instructors. You won't have much contact with your prof in one of these places; you'll just be a number. You don't want that, do you? While great things can happen on large campuses, many students will find the experience lonely and alienating.

We want Canadian students to think very carefully about small-campus alternatives. Brandon University and the University of New Brunswick at Saint John offer excellent student support and are good starting points for those who are anxious about the transition to academic work or who have weak high school records. Bishop's has perhaps the best campus life in the country and great student-oriented facilities, and its location in the Eastern Townships in Quebec makes it a very special place. Acadia, St. Francis Xavier, and Mount Allison offer first-rate educational and social experiences. UNBC is high-energy, entrepreneurial, and strongly connected to its northern setting. What small institutions lack in star appeal and magnificent buildings, they often make up in accessibility, friendliness, and support for students. Students at small universities usually speak warmly about the experience, making friends and developing a strong bond to the institution.

LOOK FOR SPECIAL FIRST-YEAR PROGRAMS

A number of Canadian universities offer dynamic first-year programs for elite students. These programs offer the best of the university experience: small classes, high-quality students, top-notch instructors, and an integrated, multi-disciplinary approach to learning. Students thoroughly enjoy these programs, which would appeal to any high school graduate with strong academic skills, a high level of intellectual curiosity, a willingness to test personal limits, and an impressive work ethic. These are not for the faint of heart. The workloads can be ferocious — but the personal, intellectual, and professional outcomes are superb. If you want to work with the best, want to be driven to be the best, and believe you have what it takes to sit with the elite students at top universities, then look at these programs. Here are some examples:

- **Arts One — UBC:** Arts One is a special program, covering eighteen of the thirty credits required in the first year of Arts study at UBC. The competitive-entry program attracts high-energy students, who apply themselves to an integrated multi-disciplinary study of history, English literature, and philosophy. The demanding program produces excellent results, and many of the students go on to great undergraduate careers. What is best about the program is its unabashed enthusiasm for the liberal arts and its conviction that demanding, high-energy, small-enrollment seminars — what used to be the foundation of the undergraduate experience — are still important in Canadian universities.

- **King's College First Year:** King's College, co-located with Dalhousie University, is one of Canada's academic gems, noted for its student-friendly atmosphere and collegial environment. The King's first-year program focuses on the "Great Books," the top intellectual achievements of humanity. Students work their way through dozens of works by the world's great thinkers, developing both a profound sense of culture and civilization and a deep analytical ability in the process. This program is a brain accelerator, designed for the top students and providing an excellent intellectual and personal return.

- **Vic One — Victoria College, University of Toronto:** Vic One was established to address the challenges of attracting top students to a large, impersonal campus. This program offers the best of the University of Toronto: elite students, superb professors, intellectually rigorous programming. Vic One is not a full academic program, but rather a sequence of elite and challenging courses that offer exceptional learning opportunities with other top students. It accepts a total of 200 students per year into six streams: the Northrop Frye Stream, the Norman Jewison Stream, the Lester B. Pearson Stream, the Egerton Ryerson Stream, the Arthur Schawlow Stream, and the Augusta Stowe-Gullen Stream. Find out what courses are on offer. If this stuff does not stir your intellectual juices, give careful thought as to whether university is really for you.

- **UC One — University College, University of Toronto:** This is a smaller version of Vic One, offering a single first-year course that focuses on Toronto's multicultural reality. The course is dynamic and exciting, and likely will stand in sharp contrast to the rest of your first-year academic experience on campus. This is precisely the kind of class that all Canadian first-year students should have available to them. Few do.

Canadian universities offer some spectacular undergraduate programs, though your guidance counsellors often do not know much about them. They are hard to get into, often requiring evidence of a lot of extra-curricular activity as well as top grades — which is one reason we recommend volunteering and work experience. These programs, however, can be life-altering. They tend to have smaller classes, intelligent classmates, top instructors, strong focus on life-long learning, excellent career potential, and true intellectual excitement. If you are a good student, highly motivated, and with a strong desire to get the most out of your undergraduate degree, give these elite programs careful attention.

CURIOSITY TEST

Chances are pretty good that you do not know all of the names of the people identified with the Vic One streams. Did you stop and check them out or did you just skim over them?

Go to the Vic One website — each of the streams is identified with a prominent Victoria College graduate or faculty member: the inventor of the laser, a pioneering female medical doctor, a director of numerous Oscar-winning films, a Nobel Prize–winning diplomat and prime minister, the educator who designed Ontario's school system, and a ground-breaking literary theorist.

Students who get into these programs rave about the educational opportunities and are impressed with the career possibilities that follow. This list is not complete, but it provides an indication of what is available for exceptional students. You will also note a pattern here. The best programs are exclusive, creating opportunities for highly skilled and hard-working students. Average and below average students, in contrast, have few such opportunities and are effectively blocked from the most interesting opportunities on campus. Some examples:

- **Arts and Science, University of New Brunswick:** The opportunity for students to complete both an arts and a science degree, typically in five years, is a real treasure. The students in this program get the best of both worlds, and leave the university with a valuable set of skills and, even better, a demonstrated capacity for wide-ranging thinking, hard work and deep curiosity.

- **Renaissance College, University of New Brunswick:** This remarkable program focuses on leadership training, giving students both a strong academic foundation and excellent opportunities to develop teamwork and leadership skills. The extra-curricular opportunities are outstanding, as is the blend of physical and intellectual activity. The program is academically rigorous, but its real strength lies in personal and professional development. (Full disclosure: Ken Coates was involved at the early stages of the planning for this program.)

- **Arts and Science, McMaster University:** This subset of the regular arts and science program is one of the best undergraduate programs in the country, drawing a great deal of interest from students, because McMaster accepts top students from this program into medical school. This is a rigorous, exciting, and wide-ranging program that attracts the best students and challenges them from beginning to end. The career outcomes of graduates have long been really impressive.

- **Knowledge Integration, University of Waterloo:** Knowledge Integration focuses on giving students the capacity to work across standard disciplinary boundaries. The work is project-based, the students and instructors are noted for their curiosity and inventiveness, and the educational experiences are first-rate. Do not let the unusual name deter you. This program provides an opportunity to broaden your academic and professional horizons. That it is connected to Canada's most entrepreneurial and career-oriented university is an added bonus.

- **Global Business and Digital Arts, University of Waterloo:** The University of Waterloo's campus in Stratford offers a unique approach to arts-based undergraduate education. There are other institutions doing digital media — Ontario College of Art and Design University in Toronto and the Great Northern Way Campus in Vancouver are also impressive — but the GBDA is quite different. It is housed in a purpose-built facility in one of Canada's most intriguing and dynamic small cities. The program has strong international connections, a prominent work-place orientation, and an emphasis on project-based learning. The connection to Canada's best-known career-preparation university is a real advantage. (More full disclosure: Ken Coates was involved in setting up this program as well.)

- **Bachelor of Humanities, College of Humanities, Carleton University:** Not all of the elite undergraduate programs focus on professional and career preparation; this program is one of the last stands of the traditional arts disciplines. The College of Humanities draws on the best in history, literature, religion, language, and cultural studies, providing a degree experience that is unabashedly enthusiastic about the intellectual traditions of the academy. This is an example of a program that is not for everyone, but that provides excellent academic opportunities for students interested in a classical approach to university education.

- **Quest University:** This is Canada's most recent attempt to create an elite liberal arts and science undergraduate institution. The university, located in Squamish, B.C., is exciting, though expensive — more than four times the average for Canada, but there are scholarships. The combination of small class size, a beautiful campus setting, the proximity to world-class skiing at Whistler, and the block program (students study one class at a time, for three and a half weeks) provide an outstanding educational experience. What's more, the university's focus on experiential learning and international participation gives the whole campus a level of creativity and engagement that is unmatched in Canada. (Still more full disclosure: Ken Coates played a minor role at the early stages of the establishment of this program.)

SEARCH OUT FIRST-YEAR TRANSITION PROGRAMS

Unless you are a top-ten (as in the number 10, not 10 percent) student at your high school, the elite first-year programs are probably not going to work for you. If you are in the bottom 50 percent, and you still end up at university despite our warnings, there are transition programs for you. Most students turn to these programs after a semester or two of academic disaster. We urgently advise you to seek them out in the first instance, especially the pre-university classes, which offer a week or so of introduction to campus life. Take the study skills seminar, the exam preparation course, and the lectures on money management.

There are special programs for English as a Second Language students, international students, students with disabilities, Aboriginal students, and even rural/small-town students. Find the programs on offer before you settle on a specific university, and take them. Ironically, many of the students who sign up for these programs are the keeners, the ones who are already set up for academic success. Students at risk, many of whom are not really sure why they are at university in the first place, generally stay away until ordered to go on threat of expulsion.

The people behind these transition and support programs really know their stuff. They have seen students at risk for many years. They know where students get tripped up, and none of your experiences will be very new to them. Dropping from A grades to D grades? Seen it many times. Struggling with your sexuality? Welcome to adulthood. Having trouble completing assignments? Join the crowd. Can't follow the lectures, and your notes don't make sense? Nothing new here. Social life on campus overwhelming your classroom work? A common experience. The academics- and support-people behind the transition programs are career-savers. They are helpful, devoted to student success, and eager to get you on the right track. The best thing you can do, if you are at risk in any way, is to meet these folks early on and follow their advice to the letter.

Once classes start, any student who is struggling should go immediately to the academic support offices. (Make sure you find them before classes start. Searching for help when you're in academic free-fall is simply too late.) If you start failing midterms, get bad grades (C or lower) on your assignments, or are not performing to your expectations (getting 75 percent when you are used to getting 90 percent is both normal in first year and extremely unnerving), seek out help. Do not wait until you have fallen behind or, worse, failed a course or, worse still, failed a whole semester. Most students at risk wait far too long. Students know if they are in trouble by the end of the first month, but most are too shy, too embarrassed, or too upset to seek help until the academic hammer descends on them, usually at the end of the semester. That is much too late.

What's at stake is not just whether or not you will be able to stay in university. It's also a matter of doing well on campus, enjoying the experience, and developing the skills you need. Cruising through to a mediocre degree is no great accomplishment. A transcript littered with failures and withdrawals is not an impressive start to your adult life.

Get help! Right away! Visit the academic support centres as soon as you get on campus. Sign up for the transition programs and learning skills classes. Attend faithfully. Pay attention! If you really apply yourself — and it's sad to think how few students take this advice and seek help only when they have already encountered serious failure — you can make up for the limitations of your high school career. Wait too long and you could well be back stocking shelves in the local supermarket before Christmas of your first year.

PICK THE RIGHT DEGREE

All of the work that has gone into picking a university can be undone by the hasty selection of the wrong academic program. This is actually the hardest part of the university selection process to get right. You have ideas about what you might like to study. Your parents are, most likely, fixated on a professional program — they love engineering, accounting, nursing, and anything that promises to be pre-med or pre-law. You could call it the "my child the doctor" syndrome.

If you look at a university calendar, the range of offerings will baffle you. Is there life after university for someone with a BA in German? What are the benefits of environmental studies? Is there more to a kinesiology degree than being a high school gym teacher? What is biotechnology? Which one of ten majors in business makes the most sense? Should you go into a direct entry program — one you enter straight out of high school, like engineering — or a more generic bachelor of arts and bachelor of science programs that delays the choice of major (your main field of study) for a year or two?

Universities offer a great deal of advising help for students struggling to decide what they want to study. Despite this, you are pretty much on your own with this one. Advisers, parents, and others can give you endless amounts of data about job opportunities, earning potential, academic and professional requirements — find out what it really takes to become a clinical psychologist before you blithely head off down that fascinating but complex and long path — but they cannot really answer the three most important questions:

- What am I really good at?

- What do I like to study?

- How can I convert this into a career at the end of my degree?

No one can really get inside your head and figure out what you enjoy doing and, even less, what you want to do as a career. Remember that, in your first year, you probably know about only a few of the jobs that might be available for you after graduation. Making a firm decision at age seventeen or eighteen, when your view of your own potential is as uninformed as is your understanding of the world of work, is absolutely *not* a good idea.

CONSIDER BIBLE COLLEGE

Bible colleges, an under-appreciated part of the Canadian post-secondary system, are the private medical clinics of the Canadian university network: they exist, but many faculty and administrators in the public system pretend that they don't. They are freestanding institutions, different from the church-based colleges on the campuses of many Canadian institutions or former church-run and now public universities that retain some of their religious character (St. FX, St. Thomas, Mount Saint Vincent, McMaster, and others started as church-controlled institutions).

For obvious reasons, Bible colleges are not for everyone. Most are based in a specific faith tradition (some being much more flexible than others in accepting people of other religious backgrounds) and expect their students to adhere to the conventions and rules of the denomination. Their programs are actually quite broad academically, but understandably have a deep connection to the study of specific religions and spiritual value systems. Some, most notably Trinity Western University in British Columbia, have extensive moral and behavioural codes that students must sign before they can be admitted.

Look at Briarcrest College in tiny Caronport, Saskatchewan, a high-quality institution that is enthusiastically embraced by its students. Look, too, at places like Crandall University (formerly Atlantic Bible College) in Moncton, New Brunswick, Redeemer University College in Hamilton, Ontario, or Canadian Mennonite University in Winnipeg, Manitoba. These are but a few of the large number of religious colleges available to you. Some offer full degrees and, in most cases (check this before you register), some of the courses you take can transfer to other universities. The Bible colleges have some of the most supportive and engaged social environments in Canadian post-secondary education. They offer a fine alternative to public institutions and are ideal for religiously active students who are not fixed on a particularly academic goal, want to enrich their religious understanding, are considering the ministry, or are looking for a comfortable, encouraging environment in which to ponder their future.

CONSIDER MILITARY COLLEGE

For those interested in a military career, Canada's military colleges are the perfect option. There are two campuses: Royal Military College of Canada in Kingston, Ontario, and Royal Military College Saint-Jean in Saint-Jean, Quebec. In both places you will be trained in our two official languages. There used to be a third, Royal Roads in Victoria, B.C., but it was converted to civilian purposes a number of years ago.

We probably don't need to sell you on the military life, because most people who choose it already know about its advantages (see the world, serve your country, a totally secure career) and its disadvantages (periodic separation from family, the possibility of dangerous service in places like Afghanistan). It's not a soft option. You have to be physically fit, and long runs and a boot-camp atmosphere are features of RMC. You won't get much sleep, particularly in your first year. Before deciding, it would be wise to talk to someone who's been through the process. You'd be smart to do some serious working out before going.

Although there is a tuition charge, it's usually waived, and officer cadets are paid a monthly salary. The RMC campuses have fairly high admission standards, and are not that easy to get into. Summer work is not only guaranteed but compulsory, and you have a firm career in the military after graduation (you have to serve for a number of years, and then you can leave if you want to). You get a first-class education in arts, science, or engineering, and your future is secure. Canada's military officers are quite well paid too: majors (eventually almost all officers will rise at least to this rank) top out at over $100,000 a year. Perhaps you will get to be a lieutenant-general, at the top of the heap. The current one makes $250,000, and everyone salutes him.

If you don't want to go to university but still find a military career attractive, you can go right into the services after high school. Here, too, the pay can be attractive: you start off at a low level, but if you have a good career you can do quite well. Warrant officers top out at around $90,000. As with RMC, there's a boot camp to go through, and you have to be fit. If the life appeals to you, you should give the military option serious consideration.

AND DON'T FORGET THESE WORDS OF ADVICE

If you choose to attend university — and you'll only know if it's the right choice for you if you do the research and are completely honest with yourself and those who care about you — then you can expect to be in for a challenging, rewarding, and life-changing experience. To make the most of this experience, we offer you this final advice (which will be applicable to the vast majority of university students):

- **Study what you love.** If you have a true passion for something, whether it is engineering or fine arts, you should seriously consider entering the field. If your parents want you to do something else, prepare yourself for difficult and lengthy talks. Arm yourself with details about work opportunities in your chosen area of study. Your naive assumption that your parents will be thrilled with your choice of Antarctic Studies will be quickly dashed, but their reaction can be offset when you demonstrate long-term and realistic thinking about the career opportunities.

- **Love what you study.** While it is valuable, at the point of entering university, to focus on long-term employability, this only works if you actually graduate with a degree in the high-employment field. Studying something like accounting, which has high academic and professional standards, is worth the effort only if you end up enjoying the work and pass the courses. There is a simple test to help you here. When you visit university campuses, stop by the bookstore. Check the textbooks assigned for the courses you would be taking in your favourite subjects. If the textbooks interest you and if you find the material fascinating, you are likely heading if the right direction. If flipping through the pages gives you a headache or makes your eyes spin, you are likely on the verge of making a bad choice.

- **Keep your options open.** While a few of the professional programs require first-year entry — where you make the selection right out of high school — most delay the final choice for a year or two. This is particularly the case in the arts and sciences, but also in most non-accredited business programs. (Accredited programs develop their curricula with advice from professional organizations and they are much more fixed and formal than most undergraduate fields.) Take advantage of the flexibility in these programs. Select your courses so that you keep your options open — this means that arts students should give serious thought to taking math and science classes in first year — and plan on spending a fair bit of time in first and second year reviewing options around the campus, and not just in the faculty or college that you entered first.

- **Prepare to work outside your field.** In most areas of study, your career options will be defined and shaped by the things you do outside of class, including volunteer activities, extra-curricular engagements, part-time work, and summer/co-op jobs. A degree in history or chemistry can be made much more powerful through the careful cultivation of your résumé and the accumulation of meaningful experiences. Do not fixate on your academic program as being the foundation for your career options. Many students who graduate with degrees in English, chemistry, environmental studies, or sociology end up with jobs outside their field of study.

- **Don't be afraid to change your major.** Students have a tendency to double down on bad program choices. Faced with overwhelming evidence that they either dislike a field of study or lack the basic aptitude for it, they will nonetheless persist, failing courses, falling behind, and, in many instances, dropping out of university. Switching programs is part of university life, and can often result in the complete transformation of your university experience. Before you jump from one degree program to another, spend some time checking out the other fields. Sit in on a few lectures in the other classes, speak to a professor or an adviser, and do some research on the subject and the career possibilities. In the end, however, you have to take the classes, complete the assignments, and sit through the examinations. Find something you like and are good at.

- **If university is not for you, leave.** We do not advise you to make quick and spontaneous decisions in this regard. Failing an assignment or a couple of midterms is not the end of the world. The transition to university is tough. Speak to an advisor or a favourite professor and talk to your parents before you jump. You might just be in the wrong program (see above). But if you find yourself skipping classes (the number-one worrying sign of intellectual disengagement), hating your assignments, panicking over examinations (pretty normal, actually), and getting terrible grades, there is a pretty good chance that you made the wrong choice when you came to university. You can wait a few months, until the university gives you a Dean's Vacation — a "go home for a semester or two" card — or you can make the choice for yourself. If the fit is really bad, and it is for close to one-third of all of the Canadian students who enroll in university, cut your costly losses early, explore other educational, training, or work options, and get on with life. University is not for everyone and, contrary to what you have been told, there are wonderful career options and high-income jobs available for people without university degrees.

We repeat: University is not for everyone, and you are not a bad person if you don't go to university, or decide to drop out if it isn't for you. The fact is, most things are not for everyone. Of your two avuncular authors, one is bored by classical music, and the other is bored by hockey — and we are both worthy people and fine citizens! Recently, a friend sent us a note about his daughter. Ponder this story (details have been changed or omitted to protect the identity of the student). She did well in high school, is smart and literate, and was pointed toward university by her extremely supportive parents, both of whom are professionals with several university degrees. They thought they had launched her on the right career path. Then a surprise:

> My daughter is in the process of switching from university (she was in Arts) to college. She was immensely unhappy at university although she didn't say much and was prepared to soldier on until we finally brought it up. She intends to get into gaming development — she wants to have a career in the digital gaming industry so she's looking for something more applied and less theoretical.

She didn't enjoy many of the rhetoric/professional writing courses. Now that this decision has been made, she is a different person. She's applied to Sheridan, George Brown and Centennial.

Smart young woman. Smart parents. Good decision. It is all about the match!

CHAPTER FOUR

THE COLLEGE OPTION

GO TO COLLEGE: THE ROAD TO EMPLOYMENT

College is often the right choice for young people graduating from high school. But while many students, particularly those who are technically inclined, attend college as a first choice, the reality is that a great many — too many — Canadians are obsessed with going to university. University is a great choice for the right student, but it should not be an automatic first option.

One of us has a son, a fine intelligent fellow who earned a BA with a major in philosophy from a university in Atlantic Canada. This led to a series of not very satisfying jobs, none of which, of course, had anything to do with philosophy — except perhaps that it helped him be philosophical about them. After a few years he decided that he was going nowhere at this, so he enrolled in a college and earned a two-year certificate in civil engineering. The maths weren't easy, and quite a few of his classmates dropped out, but he worked hard and earned his qualification. He then got a job as a project manager with a large construction firm overseas that did paving and similar contracts with the government. Five years later he is the district manager, earning six figures. University made him learned, perhaps, but college made him employable.

University graduates take note: college may be a highly attractive and relevant option for you. An increasing number of university graduates are choosing to attend college after receiving their bachelor's or master's degree. They enjoyed university, learned a great deal, absorbed the terrific educational experience that university boosters like to talk about. But their degree did not lead them into the kind of career they wanted, so they went to a college to learn a practical skill.

As you contemplate your future, we want you to give careful attention to colleges and polytechnics. If you are interested in a practical career, and are looking for a program of study that produces career-ready graduates, then colleges and polytechnics have a great deal to offer.

COLLEGE, POLYTECHNIC, UNIVERSITY: KNOW THE DIFFERENCE

Colleges and polytechnics don't have the status or prestige of universities. You can see it in the facilities. Top universities have magnificent old-style buildings and fancy new ones, often adorned with the names of donors, that say "big-name architect designed me." Their laboratories are among the best in the world, their libraries impressive, and their recreational facilities top-notch. For provincial governments, universities are show-pieces of prosperity and commitment to excellence.

Colleges and polytechnics are more practical places. Not for these institutions the soaring foyers, public art, and spiffy architecture that characterize many university campuses. This is beginning to change: there are impressive new college and polytechnic buildings, of which George Brown College's brilliant Toronto waterfront health science campus is perhaps the most spectacular. But the Saskatoon campus of the Saskatchewan Institute for Applied Science and Technology (SIAST) is more typical. SIAST is a great and well-proven training centre, but the buildings look like a large-scale high school from the 1960s. A few kilo-metres away, the University of Saskatchewan is one of the most beautiful campuses in the country, with magnificent early-20th-century buildings surrounding a student-friendly campus.

We urge you to look past the buildings, ignore the traditional Canadian attitudes about colleges and polytechnics, and see what training and skills opportunities they provide. For many Canadians, turning away from universities is a real challenge. We urge you to consider doing this. Your future might well depend on your review of these alternatives.

So, to start, let's define the difference between the institutions. The Association of Canadian Community Colleges groups more than 135 institutions that define themselves as community colleges, institutes, and polytechnics. Here is what it says about its members:

Colleges and institutes are the advanced skills educators of choice.

Advisory Committees comprising local employers align programs with their employment opportunities and ensure that colleges operate on the leading edge of skills identification, economic trends, and market shifts.

College graduates transition to employment quickly and effectively: 90% are working within 6 months.

They support business growth and sustainability by supplying graduates with advanced skills, re-skilling displaced employees, offering customized education, and providing applied research and development support.

Colleges and polytechnics are often lumped together, but there is a difference. Colleges are non-degree-granting institutions that focus on shorter, less-technological programs, while polytechnics offer diplomas and full degrees, emphasizing programs of study — in medical fields, animation, digital technologies, and the natural resource sector, among others — that require more intensive study. But while polytechnics award degrees, they don't have the basic research and broad education that you will find in a university. We deal with colleges in the remainder of this chapter, and we discuss polytechnics in chapter 6.

It should be noted that a number of polytechnics started out as colleges, and developed into polytechnics as they expanded and upgraded what they had to offer. They continue to provide college-type programs along with the more advanced polytechnic programs. So don't be surprised if you find the kinds of programs described in this chapter at a polytechnic as well as at a college.

UNDERSTAND WHAT COLLEGES HAVE TO OFFER

In Canada, which has one of the world's best networks of community colleges, the word *college* usually refers to non-degree-granting institutions, typically focused on local and regional student populations. This is confusing, because in the United States, some "colleges" are really universities that offer degrees (Dartmouth College is one of many).

Some Canadian universities contain "colleges" — the University of Toronto has University College, Western University has Huron College, and so on — but these are subsidiary units of the universities. We use *college* here to mean institutions such as Mohawk College, College of New Caledonia, Yukon College, the College of the North Atlantic, and the like.

The colleges offer a large range of programs, from adult basic education to university transfer courses (in British Columbia), but they generally don't offer degrees (some offer "applied degrees"). College students can select from the trades (brick and stone mason, electrical technician, heavy-equipment operator), paraprofessional programs (legal assistant, office manager, bookkeeper), and social service and health care studies (early childhood care worker, social work assistant, practical nurse), among others. Some colleges offer specialized career programs, such as aircraft maintenance engineering at Northern Lights College in Dawson Creek, B.C.

The colleges, most of which operate a network of small campuses, emphasize accessibility and low cost, allowing people to study close to home, restart their education, and adjust their careers. Some colleges cover large areas: Northern College's four campuses serve a 150,000-square-kilometre catchment area in northern Ontario, while Yukon College is a thirteen-campus operation with an impressive track record in Aboriginal training. By contrast, Red Deer College serves a much more focused area in central Alberta, and has done an excellent job over the years in preparing students for either the regional workforce or for further education. Saskatchewan has a system that operates through a network of seven regional colleges operating in twenty-seven communities across the province. The regional colleges do not offer programs of their own, but rather bring in programs from the University of Saskatchewan and other colleges and universities.

So colleges are close to home and inexpensive, and many (by no means all) programs are easy to get into — this is a good and bad thing, allowing almost everyone a chance but producing classes of mixed ability and motivation. They are excellent places to start and restart an education and to test out careers and training opportunities. The faculty and staff members are strongly committed to student success, and there are thousands of happy stories of previously unfocused young adults who discover their purpose in life by starting at the college level. Their programs are generally respected by employers, so they provide good access to entry-level careers. Most are little known outside their immediate area — perhaps you haven't heard of Nunavut Arctic College, with campuses in Iqaluit and elsewhere in the territory, or Confederation College in northwestern Ontario — but are usually highly regarded within their zone of activity.

MAKE SURE YOUR PICTURE OF COLLEGES IS UP TO DATE

Thirty years ago, when the parents of today's teenagers were in high school, community colleges had fairly low prestige. In those days, high school graduates often found high-paying, secure jobs in manufacturing, construction, mining, or forestry that provided solid middle-class lives. The colleges were small, well-meaning, and intensely local. They offered good technical programs that provided solid training — welding, auto mechanics, and the like. They weren't particularly prestigious, and were not ashamed of being essentially blue-collar institutions.

They are not like this anymore. Many colleges have high-end training facilities, offering the best equipment and preparation for highly technical fields. The programs train key support personnel for the professions such as nursing, dentistry, law, and engineering, often supported by professional standards and accreditation requirements. Employers have direct pipelines to the campuses and count on the colleges to provide a steady flow of career-ready graduates into their companies.

Colleges have done a better job than most universities in keeping abreast of changes in the local and regional economies — universities tend to consider themselves above such vulgar economic concerns, or at least they did until provincial governments started to squeeze their budgets. They also adapt on a regular basis to the expansion and contraction of the local workforce, dropping and adding programs as required. The programming flexibility can be hard on staff, but are appreciated by local companies and agencies seeking employees connected to the latest technical and professional developments.

Canadian colleges tend to reflect their communities in ways that universities usually do not. Rather than trying to develop a standard set of programs, as the universities do, colleges vary widely in structure and in academic and training offerings. The College of the North Atlantic is a fine school for Newfoundland and Labrador (and, oddly, for Qatar in the Middle East), but is considerably different from Assiniboine College in Brandon or the multi-campus New Brunswick Community College. While many standard elements are in place — adult basic education, health care, mechanics, and the like — there are many region-specific programs and efforts to adapt to changing local circumstances.

Colleges pride themselves on the employment experience of their graduates. Their programs focus on two things:

- Providing students with opportunities to upgrade their high school training and prepare for more specialized study.

- Offering career-ready programs tied to the local or regional economy. Colleges do very well in this area, for they usually have very close ties to the business community and expand and contract programs in line with local employment opportunities.

Despite all the public talk about the high-tech economy, a large number of jobs require less than a university degree. Two years of focused study can — and often do — provide access to a good job in the service industries, health care, social services, business, or the trades, or in certain technological fields such as civil engineering.

IF YOU'RE A UNIVERSITY GRADUATE, BE PREPARED TO GO TO COLLEGE

As noted at the beginning of this chapter, one of the most interesting trends in recent years has been the steady increase in the number of university graduates moving from the university campus to a college or polytechnic. According to Colleges Ontario, the last few years have seen a 40 percent increase in the number of university graduates attending Ontario colleges.

What is going on? These students have just spent four or more years and tens of thousands of dollars on a university education. Many have discovered — some quickly and others more painfully — that their degree did not provide a pathway to a decent job. So with varying amounts of enthusiasm, these university graduates head to a college for a career-ready position. Understandably, for most of these students, the need to go to college to round out a university education is an unwelcome surprise.

These university-college students, however, do often achieve their (changed) expectations. When the lofty professional career they had gone to university to prepare for did not materialize, they wisely changed direction and looked for a more practical preparation. For many, it was difficult to shift from a long-term plan to be a doctor, lawyer, or teacher and to become, instead, a dental technician, designer, or child care worker.

These students are often excellent classmates — highly motivated, determined to finish as quickly as possible, very focused, and good in school. They are also four or five years older than students who have come directly from high school, and bring a level of maturity to their studies. Having been burned once — and many of them see it that way — they approach their work with a determination that often exceeds that of most new college students.

The university-college transition is an important part of the Canadian education and training system. It provides university graduates with an opportunity to restart their post-secondary education, sometimes with a few credits in hand toward their diploma or degree. That university graduates

FROM UNIVERSITY TO COLLEGE TO JOB

A student graduated from a central Canadian university with a degree in political science. He loved the academic study and did well in his classes. But he had no luck on the job market, and was deeply depressed about his inability to find work.

Reluctantly, he enrolled in a short course at a college to learn how to drive large trucks and buses. Within a month of completing the program, he got a job in northern Canada, with a starting salary of $80,000 a year. He is satisfied with the new job — he does not exactly love it, nor is it what he expected when he graduated from high school — but he has a good salary and benefits and a secure position.

He is bit ticked that when Statistics Canada matches his education (highest degree: Bachelor of Arts) with his salary, he will show up as an example of "academic success." He knows differently. It is his specialized skill, determination, reliability, and work ethic that got him the job and that keep him employed. His degree? He credits academic study with making him a more informed citizen. Maybe that's enough.

cycle through college is a testament to the practical and career orientation of the community colleges — and something of a statement about the shortcomings of the universities as a training ground for workers in the contemporary economy.

INVESTIGATE CAREFULLY TO SELECT THE RIGHT COLLEGE

As we have said, Canadian students are remarkably unimaginative in their choice of institutions. Students who opt to go to college typically look in their backyard and spend little time considering opportunities elsewhere in their province, let alone in other parts of the country. This is a major mistake.

Although students searching for run-of-the-mill programs are probably well served at their local community college, there are many possibilities further afield. The national college system has a great range of options and opportunities, many of them tied to the specific historical and economic characteristics of their communities. Students interested in maritime careers should look at the College of the North Atlantic, while those preparing for jobs in the oil and gas sector would do well to consider several of the colleges and institutes in Alberta, including Keyano Community College in Fort McMurray. Fanshawe College in London, Ontario, has excellent offerings in filmmaking and new media. New Brunswick Community College in Saint John has long offered cutting-edge information technology programs.

If you are a high school graduate considering the college option, you should approach your decision this way:

- If you are looking for a standard college program available almost anywhere (the building trades, cook, dental assistant, and the like), then the local college is probably as good a choice as any, if for no other reason than that the cost of attendance is much lower than the alternatives.

- If you are planning a more specialized career, you can probably find a college program attached to your particular area of interest, but you need to take a national perspective on the search for the right school. There are thousands of college programs available across the country, many of then connected to very specific job opportunities and fields of work.

PICK THE RIGHT PROGRAM FOR YOU

Selecting a college over the other options available to you is only the start of the process. Each college has a vast array of program offerings. Let's look at a single example. Lakeland College straddles the boundary between Alberta and Saskatchewan. The regional economy is built around agriculture and the energy sector, providing excellent career prospects for well-trained graduates. The college has campuses in Vermilion and Lloydminister, Alberta, with a total of 7,500 students. The programs listed below reflect the strengths of the local economy while providing university credit courses for students considering later transfer to a university.

PROGRAMS OFFERED
BY LAKELAND COLLEGE

Academic Upgrading

Agricultural Sciences
> *Agribusiness; Animal Health Technology; Animal Science Technology; Crop Technology; General Agriculture; Veterinary Medical Assistant; Western Ranch & Cow Horse*

Business
> *General Business Major; Accounting Major; Appraisal and Assessment Major; Marketing Major; Small Business & Entrepreneurship Major; Accounting Technician; Bachelor Degrees; Agribusiness*

Continuing Education

Adult Development; Agriculture; Business; Computer Skills; Fast Track Programming; Fire & Emergency Services; General Interest; Health & Human Services; Online Learning; Performing Arts; Trades & Technology

Pesticide Applicator & Commercial Dispenser

Energy & Petroleum Technology

Heavy Oil Operations Technician; Heavy Oil Power Engineering; Gas Process Operator (GPO); Power Engineering

Environmental Sciences

Bachelor of Applied Science: (Environmental Management); Conservation & Restoration Ecology (CARE) Major; Environmental Conservation Reclamation Major; Environmental Monitoring & Protection Major; Wildlife & Fisheries Conservation Major; Renewable Energy & Conservation Certificate & Diploma

Fire & Emergency Services

Emergency Medical Technician (EMT); Emergency Services Technology (EST); Firefighter (NFPA Standard 1001)

Health & Wellness

Esthetician; Health Care Aide; Pre-employment Hairstylist

Human Services

Child and Youth Care; Early Learning & Child Care; Educational Assistant

Interior Design

Interior Design Technology

Trades & Technology Apprenticeship
Automotive Service Technician; Carpenter; Electrician; Heavy Equipment Technician; Gasfitter; Instrument Technician; Parts Technician; Steamfitter-Pipefitter; Welder

Trades & Technology Pre-employment
Pre-employment Electrician; Pre-employment Hairstylist; Pre-employment Instrument Technician; Pre-employment Welding; Street Rod Technologies

University Transfer*
Bachelor of Arts; Bachelor of Commerce; Bachelor of Education (Elementary); Bachelor of Education (Secondary); Bachelor of Science; Bachelor of Science (Agricultural/Food Business Management); Bachelor of Science (Agriculture); Bachelor of Science (Animal Health); Bachelor of Science (Environmental & Conservation Sciences); Bachelor of Science (Human Ecology); Bachelor of Science (Medical Laboratory); Bachelor of Science (Nursing); Bachelor of Science (Nutrition/Food Science)/Pre-Nutrition; Bachelor of Social Work; Pre-dental Hygiene; Pre-dentistry; Pre-medicine; Pre-pharmacy; Pre-veterinary Medicine

*courses that count for a degree awarded by a university

Multiply this impressive list of programs by the more than 130 colleges across the country, many of them offering diploma and certificate connected to the local economy, and you will have a sense of the career preparation opportunities available through the colleges.

Colleges match students with career programs by adjusting their offerings with shifts in the economy and job market. Even better, the practical nature of the diploma programs typically means that students get hands-on experience in the field before graduation. It is much easier to shift gears while still in a two-year college than it is to devote four years of university study to a field before determining whether you actually like it.

Of course, students looking at college must spend time exploring the programs — and the jobs associated with the work — before enrolling. It is easy to find out about career opportunities, including employers, salaries, job openings (locally, regionally and nationally), and related issues. Once the possibilities are narrowed down, it helps to shadow someone working in the field to get a more direct sense of what working in the field is like. Count on this: the lovely descriptions in the college catalogues are often quite different from the experience on the job. It's the experience, not the college promotional material, that will determine whether you like the work or not.

> ### IF YOU SLEPT THROUGH HIGH SCHOOL
>
> If you're wondering about the value and impact of community colleges, visit the graduating class of an adult basic education class. Adult basic education and upgrading provide opportunities for people who need to get the fundamentals down pat in preparation for a better job, including many middle-aged people who have been laid off and are unable to find work in their fields.
>
> These same programs offer a lifeline to young adults who failed in high school — often for social reasons more than because of academic or intellectual problems. If you are in this situation, we are sorry you wasted your high school years, and good for you for making the decision to get back on track. You are lucky that the colleges are around and that these programs offer a realistic, though sometimes difficult, second chance at a good career.

DON'T DISMISS PRIVATE CAREER COLLEGES

While government and parental attention focuses largely on government-funded colleges (and polytechs and universities), tens of thousands of Canadian students know that there are hundreds of other options available through private career colleges. These schools focus on direct career preparation, pride themselves on offering quick and effective instruction, and attempt to prepare students for very specific job opportunities. They often cost more than public institutions, but often offer faster routes to completion. In the main, they are no-nonsense, practical, no-frills kinds of places. Forget the football teams, choirs, residences, and well-stocked libraries. These are applied institutions, designed to move you quickly into the workforce. They open and close programs in line with the needs of the local and regional labour market and are fast-moving where public institutions are much slower to change.

The private colleges offer a great variety of programs: bookkeeping, homeopathic medicine, animation, hairdressing, office management, and many more. Much of the training — but not all of it — is focused on the lower end of the wage and career development scale. Some of these colleges are part of major Canadian and international corporate networks — Academy of Learning, Sprott-Shaw College, Trillium College, Everest College of Business, Technology and Health Care, MC College, to name only a few of the educational chains — with outlets in several cities and provinces.

We cannot begin to cover the diversity of options available in the private colleges, any more than we can do justice to the opportunities in the public colleges. The website of the National Association of Career Colleges[1] and the list of publicly licensed institutions maintained by the Canadian Information Centre for International Credentials[2] will give you a quick sense of what is on offer across the country. Some of these programs are expensive and multi-year in length. Others are cheap — and of questionable quality. One of Ken's sons, having managed to find himself on a mailing list from one "college," ticked a few boxes on a postage-paid postcard and sent it back. Within a week, he was the proud recipient of an official letter confirming his acceptance into a "challenging and prestigious" program in floral arranging. He was twelve years old at the time.

This has not been the only problem associated with private career colleges. Every once in a while, there are stories about poorly qualified instructors, facilities that fail to match the nice pictures in the brochures, and difficulties with graduate transitions to the workforce. There have also been shutdowns, sometimes in mid-semester. Several colleges set up in various Canadian cities to capitalize on the dot-com boom ran short of students and funding and closed up shop. Even as established and successful an institution as the DeVry Institute of Technology's Calgary campus closed in 2013.

But these problems by no means represent the whole. The vast majority of the private career colleges are professionally run, reliable, and focused on niche training, matching students with what are expected to be real jobs. Governments monitor and regulate the colleges, with the reporting requirements increasing in response to the highly publicized controversies. In an odd twist, a small, unlicensed operator in Ontario attracted media attention because of the high rate of employment among students who studied to become Web developers. The news reports caught the eye of government officials who visited the company, discovered that they were offering educational programs, and ordered them to close until they secured a proper license.

For adults looking to shift careers, or teenagers looking for a saleable entry-level skill, the Canadian career colleges can provide excellent opportunities. One of the best and most effective job-oriented post-secondary institutions in the country, the Vancouver Film School, is in this category. VFS focuses on animation, and declares itself "the world's best visual effects and animation studio." That is far from being an empty claim, for its faculty and graduates have the Emmys and Oscars to back it up! Anyone who automatically dismisses Canadian career colleges would miss out on this real gem — and it is not the only one in the country. So, as you consider your options, particularly if you are considering college, cast your eyes broadly across the Canadian system and make sure you include both private and public institutions.

CHAPTER FIVE

POLYTECHNICS

UNDERSTAND THE POLYTECHNICS' UNIQUE MISSION

Of all the post-secondary options in the country, the most effective in preparing graduates for employment are the polytechnics, perhaps the most under-appreciated institutions in Canada. Most Canadians lump colleges and polytechnics together, a perspective that ignores the unique mission and special status of the country's eleven polytechnics. These post-secondary institutions are large, growing, well connected to industry and business, obsessed with the career outcomes of their graduates, and of impressively high quality.

Here is how Polytechnics Canada — the association established to promote this sector to students, the public, business, and governments — describes its member institutions:

> **The Polytechnic Advantage: a high-quality, job-focused education**
>
> **Formula for success: a three-pronged approach to creating jobs and supporting industry**
>
> 1. Strength in academic offerings
>
> 2. Strength in industry connections
>
> 3. Strength in applied research

Polytechnics Canada members develop the highly qualified people essential to the Canadian economy by:

- providing career-focused and community-responsive education developed in partnership with employers (87 percent of graduates were employed within six months of graduating);

- committing to a wide range of credentials, including bachelor degrees, diplomas, apprenticeships, certificates, post-graduate offerings, continuing education and corporate training, spanning many fields;

- combining theoretical and applied learning, relevant work experience for students and the opportunity for them to participate in applied research and commercialization projects; and

- offering pathways that allow students to build on their credentials, recognizing previous learning.

Polytechnics are career-focused, offering practical training developed in co-operation with employers and strongly influenced by advanced applied research. Because of their high quality, they usually attract many more applications for popular programs than they can fill. As a result, the applied teaching and research profile of the polytechnics has begun to get increasing attention from the public sector and more money from governments. Like the colleges, they are often highly attractive options for people who already hold degrees. If you are one of these people, you should look very closely at the polytechnics.

The eleven official members of Polytechnics Canada are: British Columbia Institute of Technology (Burnaby); Southern Alberta Institute of Technology Polytechnic (Calgary); Northern Alberta Institute of Technology (Edmonton); Saskatchewan Institute of Applied Science and Technology (Saskatoon); Red River College (Winnipeg); Humber

POLYTECHNICS STILL DON'T HAVE THE RESPECT THEY DESERVE

In recent years, polytechnics have begun to take on several of the key characteristics of universities, offering full degrees (but with much more focused courses), securing government research funding, and building stronger connections with government and the private sector. But the polytechnics are fundamentally different in function and design, tied closely to the needs of local employment markets, especially in the private sector. It is vital that polytechnics maintain their distinct identity and mission — even as the number of institutions and students continues to grow.

To date, Canadians have not fully embraced polytechnics, despite the career successes of their students and their engagement in economic development. Parents and high-school graduates are still obsessed with universities. Although this bias is changing somewhat, politicians still tend to favour universities over colleges and polytechnics in their planning and financial allocations. This is a real shame.

College Institute of Technology and Advanced Learning (Toronto); Algonquin College (Ottawa); George Brown College (Toronto); Conestoga College Institute of Technology and Advanced Learning (Kitchener); Seneca College (Toronto); and Sheridan College Institute of Technology and Advanced Learning (Oakville). They all have satellite operations and are not confined to a single location.

Polytechnics are regional in coverage, but noticeably absent in Quebec and the Atlantic Provinces. (Do note that polytechnic-type programs are offered through universities, particularly Dalhousie University, which amalgamated with the former DalTech in 1997, and that professional programs are offered by the CEGEPs in Quebec and the regional colleges in the Atlantic Provinces.) They are career-oriented, high-technology and professionally focused, and deeply engaged with national and international businesses. Polytechnics are not designed to be easy to get into — they are as committed as the top universities to excellence, and do not have the open-access policy of the colleges. They offer the most practical education and training system available in Canada.

DON'T GO TO A POLYTECHNIC FOR AN EASY RIDE

You know that we admire colleges and universities, and these institutions will continue to offer high school graduates fine options. But if you're looking for a post-secondary education that is designed to link you directly with the workforce, then the polytechnics are the strongest choice for the twenty-first century. But you must have some focus, for these are not places for people who don't know what they want to do. They look for highly motivated, energetic students with the background and skills needed to succeed in what are often very technical or scientific fields. Check out the Bachelor of Applied Technology Petroleum Engineering at the Southern Alberta Institute of Technology (SAIT) or Sheridan's popular program in Computer Animation (Digital Character Animation). These are high-quality, industry-tested programs, targeted specifically to the career opportunities in their respective fields.

The special character of the polytechs is captured nicely in Sheridan's Computer Animation promotional material: "Sheridan's instructors, all longtime veterans of the industry, will do more than work with you on your skills. They'll also teach you good work habits as well — the little things that can make the difference between mediocre work and outstanding character computer animation." These places are not like high schools, where the priority appears to be making you feel good about yourself, or university, where the less hands-on standards of the lifetime academic are applied. Polytechs get students ready for business, both by providing the skills training and by introducing them to the pressures, conditions, expectations, and demands of the modern workplace.

If universities were on top of the employment realities of the 1970s and 1980s, the torch has now passed to the polytechnics and, to a lesser degree, the colleges. These institutions offer practical education for a practical age. They provide a range of certificate, diploma, and degree options, have strong ties with employers, and offer solid employment prospects for graduates. They are well connected to contemporary technological realities and offer students excellent laboratories and training facilities. Their degree programs, in particular, are intensive and highly focused, with a strong emphasis on project and personal work. Many of the polytechs now offer a range of four-year degree programs — some university people don't like this much — and many of these programs are gaining a real foothold in the marketplace, particularly in terms of prestige and status.

Studying at a polytechnic is not an easy ride. Precisely because they are so well connected to the workforce and employers, they know that their graduates are expected to make a rapid transition from study to paid employment. The teachers and programs are demanding and very results-oriented. In many of the programs, the approach to learning copies a lot from the paid workforce, particularly in attention to deadlines, specifications, and client service. In short, you can't goof off there and hope to succeed. Polytechnics are not for the swarm.

MAKE SURE YOU HAVE FOCUS AND COMMITMENT

We asked you before to do a full and honest assessment of yourself. If you are unsure of your commitment to a specific technical or professional field, you would be better off taking a more general practical education in a college or a more open-ended academic course of study at a university (or, even better, taking time away from advanced studies until you are ready to make a real decision). Colleges and universities are better suited for people uncertain of their career path and interested in exploring options. Polytechnics demand, and get, more focus and more commitment. Give them careful attention if you are practical, want a well-paid job after you are finished your studies, are comfortable with technical work, and possess a strong work ethic.

We have told you, repeatedly, that the job market is tough and getting tougher. But there are actually many jobs out there — well-paid, dependable, and practical jobs. Many of the most lucrative positions are technology-based, requiring a combination of intelligence, creativity, and practical ability. Employers are constantly complaining about their inability to find the right workers for the most urgently needed positions. While they carry no guarantee of employment — no one knows what the next decade will bring — the polytechnics are the most promising route to those jobs.

Here is another fact — and potentially an unhappy one. Many of the top programs at the polytechnics are hard to get into. Some, like those for dental technicians, can have years-long waiting lists. Unlike universities, which can always squeeze more students into a five-hundred-student classroom, most polytechnic programs can handle only a fixed number of students, with the limits set by the facilities, the work placements, and the need for instructors to provide individualized instruction. They work to align their programming with the marketplace and thus take care not to flood the workforce with too many graduates.

Getting admitted to Sheridan's superb animation program — to select only one example of dozens — is harder than getting into most of the universities in the country. Many of the medical technology, digital design, and career-ready programs have hundreds of students trying to get in. In fact, many university graduates are among those competing for entry-level spots in the polytechnic programs. While the polytechnics are among the best-kept educational secrets in the country, a growing number of young people have figured them out.

LOOK FOR THE BEST POSSIBLE MATCH

Polytechs work for another reason. They are closely attuned to the changes in the Canadian economy, right down to the level of individual programs. While universities have no compunction about producing thousands of surplus psychology graduates ("Let the students decide") and while colleges graduate a steady stream of heavy equipment operators, hair-dressers, and other skilled workers ("Career preparation is our specialty"), the polytechs work more closely with the business community and government to determine actual workplace demand. While they do not always get it right — some polytech graduates do have trouble finding work in their chosen field — they try a lot harder than universities do.

The polytechs talk routinely with business — benefiting by getting access to the best pieces of technology so that graduates are ready to make a smooth jump from their studies into the world of work — and adjust their program intakes on the basis of declared industry need. Trying to maintain a match between the production of graduates and workforce requirements is a hallmark of polytech planning. We hope that they resist the pressure from students and governments to focus — as colleges and universities do — on meeting student demand rather than workforce needs. They will be sorry if they go down that path, the one that has severely undercut the utility of general arts and sciences programs.

It is time for parents, in particular, to understand the enormous potential and opportunities that rest in the polytechnics. The question is not "Which institutions are the best?" but rather "Which institution and what program is best for this particular student?" At this point, Canadians focus on the first question and largely ignore the second. Parents, guidance counsellors, and institutional recruiters need to help you, as a high school graduate, to shift your focus and search for the best possible match, rather than following the swarm to the supposedly most prestigious institution. Your career depends on it.

EXPECT A HANDS-ON EXPERIENCE

The polytechs specialize in moving students into work-type settings quickly. While there is classroom work in even the most technical programs, students generally spend a lot of time in laboratories, machine rooms, or other simulated workplace environments. Polytechs typically require students to do a lot of project and team work, to complete personal projects, and to connect classroom tasks with workplace experience.

Importantly, this applies to the polytechs' research activity as well. A growing number of faculty members at the polytechs manage research projects, most of them co-sponsored by business and industry. The basic, curiosity-based research that dominates universities is not much in evidence here. Because the polytechs do not have graduate students (although that will change soon and is partly underway), undergraduate students end up working on many of these projects. The opportunity to participate in major company- or industry-focused research projects is a huge advantage to a diploma or degree program. It is an over-simplification to say that polytech and college students learn by doing while university students talk about their subjects: many university programs, from digital arts to engineer and nursing, have a lot of practical elements. In the polytech world, however, practical, hands-on experience is fundamental to the programs and, therefore, to student preparation.

One of the implicit commitments the polytechs have with employers is that the graduates of their practical and applied programs will be career-ready when they leave the institutions. Contrast this with a 2013 editorial by Wilfrid Laurier University President Max Blouw, who argued the opposite: that businesses had to take a much more active role in preparing university graduates for jobs. In the current environment, where companies feel under enormous pressure to hire people who can move quickly and effortlessly into the workforce, President Blouw's commentary simply reinforced the general notion that universities were not connected to workplace realities. We have never heard a polytech president make such a claim. Indeed, the opposite is true, with the polys routinely asking the business community how they can best adapt their curriculum and practical training to prepare better the students for jobs.

PREPARE CAREFULLY BEFORE APPROACHING A POLYTECHNIC

So, how do you approach a polytech? It is not a simple question. The country's preoccupation with universities is so strong that parents, students, and counsellors are used to standard structures (faculties and colleges) and programs (arts, science, business, medicine). Polytechs do not work the same way, and it requires more intensive investigation and planning to benefit from attending one. When you check out universities, you will typically find that the first year is devoted to general studies — in the arts, science, or business — with the final decision about the primary field of study postponed until second or even third year. This is a strength of universities, for it works on the assumption that students need a fair bit of time on campus to understand both program and career options, to experiment with familiar and brand new areas of study, and to discover their passion. Students who come to university to study in the arts might take courses in such diverse areas as history, biology, German, economics, and psychology in the first semester alone and could easily end up shifting their planned major 180 degrees from where they started.

While polytechs allow shifting and refocusing, they assume that students have prepared carefully for their advanced study and have a good idea of what they want to learn. But here is the polytech trick: their programs are different, the range of opportunities is much greater, and they are best suited for young adults with a real sense of purpose that focuses on a practical career. Like universities, they are not for everyone. In fact, one of the things we worry about is that the greater career success enjoyed by polytech graduates will lead the swarm to shift their focus from universities to polytechs, reproducing the overcrowding and overproduction of graduates that has become the hallmark of the university system. So, do yourself a favour. Don't rush off to a polytech simply because it is more attuned to the realities of the twenty-first-century economy. Check it out carefully — and, as we constantly urge you to do, test what you see against your abilities, your passions, and your interests in life.

LOOK TO POLYTECHS FOR A REGIONAL FOCUS

When you do this, what will you see, other than post-secondary institutions that are quite different than universities? Let's take a quick look at two of this country's polytechs: Sheridan College, headquartered in Oakville and with four campuses in southern Ontario, and Northern Alberta Institute of Technology (NAIT), a career-focused institution based in Edmonton and connected to the red-hot economy in Alberta.

Sheridan is known internationally for its digital media programs, but its career preparation offerings have a much greater reach than that. The impressive range of programs shown here — and all of the major institutions have dozens of programs — is only a partial list of diploma, degree, and certificate options at Sheridan, most of them with a very specific career focus. NAIT — along with its Calgary counterpart, SAIT — is highly regarded for its ability to prepare students for high-demand careers. While there is some overlap with Sheridan, the Ontario polytechnic's programs reflect the structure of the southern Ontario manufacturing and service economy while NAIT's offerings are focused on the resource-based, rural, and specialized industrial economy of Alberta and the west.

Now, do a test. Consider two comparable universities — say McMaster University in Hamilton and the University of Alberta in Edmonton. When you review their degree offerings, you will see that there is a great deal of duplication, probably as much as 90 percent of the programming. Where the polytechs are designed to respond to serve regional markets while offering certificates, diplomas, and degrees that are recognized nationally and internationally, universities offer degrees that are more generic in nature. The majority of the degree offerings at McMaster are the same as the ones at Alberta, and everywhere else for that matter, with some specialization (Alberta offers agriculture, for example, and there are specializations within engineering and some other fields that reflect regional needs).

PROGRAMS OFFERED BY SHERIDAN COLLEGE INSTITUTE OF TECHNOLOGY AND ADVANCED LEARNING

Bachelor's degrees (selected)
- Art and Art History
- Animation
- Game Design
- Interaction Design
- Illustration
- Interior Design
- Music Theatre Performance
- Photography
- Global Business Management
- Athletic Therapy
- Exercise Science and Health Promotion
- Information Systems Security
- Computing and Network Communications
- Design
- Communication, Culture and Information Technology
- Early Childhood Technology
- Theatre and Drama Studies
- Applied Computing (Mobile Computing)

Ontario College Diplomas (selected)
- Advertising and Marketing Communications
- Architectural Technicians
- Business Administration
- Chemical Laboratory Technician
- Community and Justice Services
- Community Worker
- Computer Engineering Technician

Computer Program
Computer Systems Technician (Software Engineering)
Early Childhood Education
Educational Support
Electromechanical Engineering Technician
Electronics Engineering Technician
Information Technologies Support Services
Interior Decorating
Investigation (Public and Private)
Journalism
Makeup for Media and Creative Arts
Mechanical Engineering Technician
Office Administration
Paralegal
Personal Support Worker
Pharmacy Technician
Police Foundations
Practical Nursing
Social Service Worker*
Technical Production for Theatre and Live Events
Tourism and Travel
Veterinary Technician
Visual and Creative Arts
Visual Merchandizing

*including Social Service Worker — Immigrant and Refugee Stream and Social Service Worker — Gerontology

PROGRAMS OFFERED BY THE NORTHERN ALBERTA INSTITUTE OF TECHNOLOGY

Subjects of study
- Animal Studies
- Building Construction and Design
- Business and Administrative
- Engineering and Applied Sciences
- Environmental Management
- Health and Safety
- Hospitality and Culinary Arts
- IT and Electronics
- Mechanical and Industrial
- Media and Design
- Recreation and Outdoors
- Trades and Upgrading

Specialized programs (selected)
- Airbrake Certification
- Auto Body Technician
- Automotive
- Blacksmithing
- Building Environmental Systems
- Computer Numerical Control
- Fluid Power Certificate
- Heavy Duty Electronics
- Heavy Equipment
- HVAC certificate
- Hydronic Designer and Installer
- Industrial Heavy Equipment
- Instrumentation Engineering

Machine Shop
Mastercam
Mechanical Engineering
Millwright
Non-Destructive Testing
Oil Field Thread Inspection
Petroleum Engineering
Power Engineering
Recreational Powersports Mechanics
Refrigeration
Steamfitter/Pipefitter
Welding

Bachelor's degrees
Applied Business Administration
Applied Information Systems Technology
Business Administration
Technology Management
Accounting
Finance

EXPECT PRACTICAL TRAINING, NOT BEAUTIFUL CAMPUSES

Because polytechs are strikingly different from universities — both in terms of their general applied focus and their emphasis on specialized programs — they should be approached very differently. University recruitment highlights campus life, residence opportunities, institutional status, and heritage. (A major exception to this generalization is found in the Waterloo region, where three impressive institutions — University of Waterloo, Wilfrid Laurier University, and one of the country's top polys, Conestoga College — share an equally unimpressive and bland architectural style. None of the institutions — all of which are great at what they do — is an aesthetic delight.) The social side of the polytechnic experience is not the equivalent of going to university. The campuses are practical, dominated by laboratories and work rooms more than leafy walkways, huge libraries, and big residence complexes. They do not highlight intercollegiate sports, have fewer and less generous donors, and lack the prestige long associated with universities. What they do provide is great preparation for the workplace, practical facilities that are often the best in the country, a sustained commitment to cutting-edge learning opportunities, and an overwhelmingly practical approach to education and training. Do you want to cheer on a university football team or train for a good practical career? Your choice.

Polytechs, like the colleges, spend less time and effort trying to recruit students, and are thus better suited to students who search them out than to those who have been drawn in by an effective video pitch, recruiting speech, or promotional campaign. The reason is simple. Unlike universities, which are largely undifferentiated, polytechs are highly specialized: they know what they are and what they offer and they make much less of an effort to attract students to their institution. Universities want you to pick them out of a crowded field. Polytechs know that they are unique and they count on the students to seek them out.

They certainly know that employers direct students their way and, on a regional basis, each of the polytechs has a strong reputation for responding to the needs of the workforce. Consider it a good part of the self-evaluation process. If you are sufficiently motivated and organized to discover the polytech that has what you want, they are likely to be keener about your application. If you need to be wooed, then you are probably not well suited to the polytech environment.

If you are practically inclined, and if preparing yourself for a specific career (often with high and steady income potential) is your top priority, you should do a detailed investigation of all relevant polytechnics. For the technically oriented, look at the applied science and technology programs. Students with a business or social service orientation will find a full range of offerings that rely much less on a high school science and mathematics background.

Most students will have little familiarity with many of the degree and diploma options. Perhaps you already know what BCIT's Cardiovascular

Perfusion program is all about, but we had to search the Internet to find out. For those who are curious, cardiovascular perfusion is

> the science of providing extra-corporeal circulation in order to artificially support and temporary replace a patient's respiratory and circulatory systems. Clinical perfusionists are expert members of the cardiac surgical team, and can be found providing life-saving support of patients requiring extra corporeal circulation, including but not limited to major cardiothoracic, vascular and transplant surgeries, as well as support of the critically-ill patient.

Along similar lines, are you familiar with the career opportunities associated with Algonquin College's Photonics and Laser program? The college's website declares:

> The growth of these diverse, but linked, optical technology based areas is inevitable and will require broadly trained professionals able to contribute to the evolution of the industry. The training required involves both a solid grounding in theory as well as a considerable level of experience in relevant hands on skills. The electronics industry, just one of the sectors dramatically affected by the growth of photonics, has previously been the driver of communication. This area has been largely and increasingly, superseded by a combination of fibre optic and wireless communication, and this shift in technology is expanding as the sharing of information increases.

Are these neat, or what?

VISIT A POLYTECHNIC

Catalogue listings tell only a small part of the story. The polytechs require more detailed investigation if you are to find the right match. You have to go well beyond perusing the website and reading the promotional material. Make sure you attend an on-campus polytech orientation night (going to the career fair is a poor second choice, as you will be speaking to recruiters and not to the professionals and specialists in the field). Look at the laboratories, drop into the bookstore and look at the course texts in the programs you are considering, and see if you can sit in on a class. Remember that Canadian institutions see you more and more as a customer than as a student and they are much better than in the past about accommodating special requests.

If you have narrowed down the field of study, see if you can examine a work site or company specializing in a particular area. These are unique and highly specialized careers, in the main, and your enthusiasm for the program is likely to be closely tied to your understanding of the career possibilities. Polytechs are best suited to students with a clear focus and an understanding of what they want out of their education and career. Unlike universities, which appropriately emphasize breadth of knowledge and the opportunity to shift direction, polytechs are very career-obsessed. If you are too, then they could easily be the perfect match.

CHAPTER SIX

VOLUNTEERING AS A LAUNCH PAD

BE PART OF THE ENGAGED MINORITY

What a contradictory lot you young people are these days! Reporters, always keen to know what you're thinking, say that you have a strong interest in helping the poor, engaging with the world, and working for social justice. The truth is, however, that many young people are far more interested in social media, video games, and earning money. This is only natural — asked to tick off your interests, you of course will choose "saving the environment" over "hoisting some brews" — even as you head off to the pub.

But you aren't all like this: for a minority of young people, engagement with community is a crucial part of their lives. They have already been actively working, through their faith communities, Boy Scouts or Girl Guides, co-operatives, environmental groups, and other agencies to better the world. These young people — and the adults who inspire them — are the backbone of society, and critical to our pursuit of social justice in our time. It is to them, and to people who might like to be like them, that this chapter is addressed.

Volunteerism, though certainly praiseworthy, is not often seen as a strong element in career building. It is viewed as a time out, a separate activity that responds to the spiritual or social justice part of a person's make-up, rather than as an integral part of personal or professional development. We wouldn't want to downplay the humanitarian zeal and the concern for others that drives the volunteer impulse. At the same time, we want to emphasize that it can be extremely valuable to your career and your adult life.

VOLUNTEER AS A WAY OF GIVING SOMETHING BACK

Let's dispense right away with the cynical approach to volunteerism as a means of puffing up your résumé. In the United States, where competition to get into the elite universities and colleges is intense, having impressive volunteer activities on your record can push your application closer to the top of the pile. Employers, too, love to see signs that there is a heart and soul behind the job experience and credentials

So, of course, a few enterprising individuals seize the opportunity to make some money from the altruism of others. There are actually companies that charge a fee to match students' interests with volunteer opportunities. They realize that their clients want to be seen helping the disadvantaged, but without getting their hands dirty or dealing with really poor or sick people. These firms, shamefully, match clients with highly visible "volunteer" opportunities — good for Facebook pages and résumés but actually accomplishing very little. At their worst, these involve staying at a high-end hotel and making brief visits to an orphanage in a developing country or an AIDS hospice so that the client can be photographed "helping" the disadvantaged. Unimpressive, to be sure, and so transparent that this system is unlikely to fool people for long — though there seems to be money to be made in it. If you hire one of these outfits to make you look good, shame on you too.

We don't want to be chauvinistic, a Canadian failing we often ascribe to the Americans, but we really are lucky to live in this country. By both historical and global standards, people in this country are among the richest in the world. Remember that there are more than a billion people who exist on less than $1 a day — less than the cost of a regular chocolate bar, or half the daily cost of your cellphone contract.

It's hard to put a firm number on the relative wealth of Canadians, but let's give it a go. Wealth is defined in many ways, most typically by individual and family income. By these standards, Canada has long ranked comfortably in the top ten countries in the world. But money in the pocket is only one measure of wealth. A wealthy person or wealthy society should be able to count on many non-monetary benefits. After all, what value is it to have stacks of money, but live in constant fear or being robbed or killed, as is the case in too many countries. So, a proper measure of "wealth" should include other factors — such as life expectancy, access to health care, educational opportunities, the status of women and children in society, safety within the home and the community, freedom from war and domestic strife, fresh water, non-polluted air, freedom from hunger, and decent shelter and clothing. By these standards, the average Canadian is probably in the top 2 percent of all of the people who have ever walked the face of the earth.

If you have any kind of social conscience, you will have to agree that our wealth carries at least some national and global obligations. (If you don't, feel free to say "whatever" and skip the next few pages, but remember that you will be missing some real rewards.) People have, arguably, an obligation to give back — through their effort or their money — to the less advantaged among them. Many Canadians feel that the federal and provincial governments handle these responsibilities at the local, regional, and national level — funded, of course, from tax revenue paid by all Canadians — and that Ottawa discharges our global responsibilities through foreign aid contributions.

The uncomfortable fact is that, in terms of proportion of Gross Domestic Product devoted to foreign aid, Canada is fourteenth on the list of donor countries at 0.32 percent; the top countries, Sweden, Norway, and Denmark, give more than 0.8 percent of GDP. Our commitment to foreign aid has never reached the internationally recommended target of 0.7 percent of GDP, and historically much of our aid has been tied to sales of Canadian foodstuffs and machinery — which of course is good for our economy. If it makes you feel better, the United States ranks considerably lower, donating about 0.19 percent of its GDP — not counting, of course, the country's vast overseas military expenditures.

It falls on individual donors and volunteers to take up the slack. Canadians often respond generously, as they did following the 2004 tsunami in Southeast Asia, the devastating 2010 earthquake in Haiti, and the 2013 typhoon in the Philippines. We respond well to the campaigns run by the Red Cross, Oxfam International, Engineers Without Borders, Free the Children (a wonderful Canadian-led charity), Médicins sans Frontierès, and hundreds of other charities. We volunteer at food banks, attend fund-raising auctions and concerts, sponsor children in the developing world, and worry about the misuse of donated funds by crooked foreign governments. Canadians are reasonably generous people, although the largest share of our tax-deductible donations goes to our faith communities, which pass some of it along in the form of foreign aid.

VOLUNTEER AS A WAY OF DISCOVERING YOURSELF

We see volunteerism as an opportunity for you to connect with people, communities, and countries much less advantaged than you may be. Volunteering carries a number of personal benefits. You will, through volunteering, develop a much greater understanding of and empathy for people who are poor, physically or mentally disabled, living with a personal or natural disaster, or otherwise struggling to make it through life. You may — particularly if you work directly with people in need (as opposed to through third-party organizations) — develop real compassion, acquired through thinking about the differences between your own life and the lives of other people who suffer through no direct fault of their own. Your appreciation for the complexities of the human condition will grow immensely if you make connections with people from other communities, countries, societies, and cultures.

By volunteering, you will test yourself in many difficult and complex ways. Dealing directly with hungry people is never easy, and it is much more challenging when you know that you will not face real privation in your life at home. The first exposure to real poverty is, for most people, a real eye-opener, upsetting their understanding of humanity and sparking a concern for social justice. Encountering wide-spread and deliberate environmental destruction, the brutal mistreatment of women, religious or cultural discrimination, massive slums, inadequate water supplies, and the like will have a profound impact on your world-view. Some of you will be unaffected and simply see your wealth and comfort as something you have earned or deserve by natural right. A significant number, though, are changed forever, and set forth on a life marked by concern for others.

Volunteering will probably not transform you into a humanitarian like Mother Teresa (who worked for decades with the poor and ill in India) or a social activist like Canada's Stephen Lewis, who has been a world leader in the battle against HIV/AIDS. Not that it would be a bad thing if you became saint-like, of course — it's just unlikely. At root, the fundamental benefit of volunteering for you is that it will make you confront yourself and draw attention to your assumptions about both your place in the world and the challenges facing the poor, the dispossessed, and the uncared for. As a bonus, it will set you apart from the swarm.

Volunteerism provides enormous opportunities for global exploration. You can work on a Habitat for Humanity project in your community, building homes for people who need basic shelter, or you can join a group working in Mozambique to build houses for women and children affected by HIV. Free the Children permits you to raise funds locally to support educational and health programs in the developing world. Craig and Marc Kielburger, founders of Free the Children, are brilliant and admirable examples of what Canadian young people can do. There are thousands of charities doing great work at the local, national, and international levels.

We want you to consider spending a few months or even a year or more volunteering before you go on to post-secondary education or into the workforce. Young people often feel real pressure to get on with life, only to head off into a field of endeavour for which they are ill suited. You are likely seventeen or eighteen years old. You are a young adult, probably with at least six decades of life ahead of you. Taking a year or two to help others is only a short detour from whatever path you choose. Volunteering can provide you with a life-changing

KATIMAVIK AND CUSO

A generation ago, Canada had a small and politically controversial attempt to prepare young people for a life of service called Katimavik (the word means "meeting place" in Inuktitut). Founded in 1977, Katimavik had good intentions but lacked effective management and eventually turned into a privately funded and much smaller undertaking. The government of Canada announced the withdrawal of federal funding in 2012, but as of 2013 Katimavik declared itself to be alive, fund-raising and planning on putting Canadians into the field as volunteers in the spring/summer of 2013. You can read about it at *www.katimavik.org*.

Perhaps a more familiar example to Canadians is CUSO, which was founded in 1961 as Canadian University Service Overseas, and now, as CUSO International, is part of a wider alliance of voluntary organizations that over the past fifty years has placed over 45,000 volunteers, about a third of them Canadian, in various countries overseas. CUSO currently has 350 volunteers working in twenty-seven developing countries for periods of between three months and two years. They particularly want people with skills that match their projects, and if you are interested, you should look at their website (*cusointernational.org*).

perspective on the world, a way of placing your options and opportunities in a broader global context. People have been doing this for generations, heading off to help in Christian mission fields at home or overseas, joining international aid organizations to provide crisis assistance in times of natural or human disaster, or, to use a well-known American example, signing up for the Peace Corps and heading off to make the world a better place.

Of course, you can always help out in your home community or region. There is never a shortage of opportunities at seniors' homes, elementary- and pre-schools, drop-in centres, agencies working with people living with mental and physical challenges, environmental organizations, and many, many others. You could easily put together a full slate of commitments without going more than a few kilometres from home, discovering opportunities to engage with local citizens and the community at large. To a degree that very few Canadian appreciate, this country runs substantially on volunteer labour, and you can do much worse than join the huge volunteer army that keeps Canada moving.

MAKE SURE THE COMMITMENT YOU CHOOSE IS RIGHT FOR YOU

You have to be careful in selecting your volunteer opportunity. Some people find it hard to see extreme poverty. Others find serious diseases upsetting. Many Canadians, raised with the uncrowded spaces and large expanses of this massive country, have trouble dealing with the huge, chaotic slums that surround major cities in the developing world.

You have to be honest about your comfort level with different cultures and communities. Canadian women, raised in the open and generally welcoming conditions in this country, can chafe at the restrictions governing their actions in fundamentalist regions and under oppressive regimes. There are many dangerous parts of the world — all of them desperately in need of volunteers and assistance — that would frighten even the bravest people. Be sensible about these things. Just imagine how your parents would react to hearing that you had decided to spend a year in Afghanistan or Yemen. You can volunteer without making a martyr of yourself or putting yourself at unnecessary risk.

VOLUNTEER OPPORTUNITIES FOR YOU TO CONSIDER

- Help out in a hospital, orphanage, or centre for children with disabilities
- Assist community-based political organizations
- Support training initiatives for dispossessed workers
- Work on agricultural projects, including local food security activities targeted at the urban poor
- Support children and families suffering from HIV/AIDS
- Teach English as a Second Language or assist in understaffed schools
- Volunteer with public health programs
- Help preserve and interpret historic sites
- Get involved in business development and micro-business activities
- Assist with youth sports and community cultural activities
- Help with environmental reclamation and conservation initiatives
- Participate in important local or international research projects
- Perform with and assist community arts organizations
- Help Habitat for Humanity complete building projects
- Support journalists and social activists with public awareness activities

Multiply the number of items on this list by the scores of countries urgently requiring assistance, many with hundreds of communities or rural areas. The world is not short of opportunities to help.

REMEMBER THAT VOLUNTEERING CAN HELP YOUR CAREER

It's not all self-sacrifice. There's a practical benefit to volunteering. The first priority should always be the opportunity to help others. From start to finish, benefits to yourself should be secondary. But it's a happy fact that properly undertaken volunteer activities can make a major contribution to your career possibilities. Admissions officers love to discover that a top student has a solid social conscience. Employers are more impressed with young people who have made a commitment to helping others than with those who spent their summers serving at McDonald's or their gap year working as a retail clerk in the downtown mall — or even backpacking around Asia, though that can be a positive experience too (see chapter 8). At a simple level, therefore, volunteering looks good on future job applications.

The career-boosting benefits of volunteering go well beyond building your résumé, important as this can be. If you have selected your volunteer activities properly — working with the poor in Guatemala looks a great deal better than helping out at the high school graduation ceremonies for an elite, expensive private school — you will have told people evaluating your file a great deal about yourself. Your volunteer activities should have several of these characteristics: longer term (four months to a year), work is clearly humanitarian or related to environmental or social justice issues, in a different cultural setting, presenting personal challenges (physical, psychological, emotional, or cultural) and providing practical experience.

The last point is crucial. Eventually, when you get back to Canada, you will want a job, either right away or after some kind of post-secondary education or training. Picture an employer reviewing two résumés, both from young people with the same level of education: university, college, apprenticeship, or just high school. One stayed at home, had several part-time, low-skill jobs, and now wants a real job. The other spent a year in South America, developed Spanish language skills, and began as a teacher in an elementary school but ended up as the manager for the local food co-operative. Remember that, as an employer, you are looking for standard employability skills in your prospective workforce. Compare a volunteer and a non-volunteer in these categories: breadth of experience, organizational skills and experience, humanitarian qualities, confidence in speaking, evidence of work ethic, commitment to personal development, professionalism, international awareness, growth potential, openness, and creativity. Which one comes out on top?

This is not to say that local or national volunteer activity is without real merit. Indeed, a full-time local volunteer will likely stand out above the crowd of young people who have had stay-at-home, low-skill jobs. But from a career-building perspective, an international engagement grabs greater attention. Everyone from family members to admissions officers and future employers is impressed that you spent half a year in the favelas in Brazil, taught in an elementary school in Ghana, built flood-control systems in Sri Lanka, or supported a major conservation effort in Nicaragua. Supporting the local food bank, volunteering with a youth sports initiative, or visiting the elderly in a hospice are all valuable activities that reflect very well on you. They simply do not generate as much spontaneous interest as a long-term international engagement.

The most crucial element of volunteering is that it opens your eyes to your own strengths and weaknesses as well as to the opportunities and challenges of the modern world. Whether you volunteer in your home community, elsewhere in Canada, or in another country, you are going to expand your horizons, learn a great deal more about the world, and enhance your future employability.

CHAPTER SEVEN

TRAVEL: DISCOVER THE WORLD

LEARN FROM THE KIWIS AND AUSSIES

We are firm believers in the importance of seeing the world. Rather than rushing off to university, college, the workplace or some other activity, many young people would benefit from leaving the country and travelling. We are not talking about a week in Florida on a spring break–type party, a month overseas on familiar territory, or a visit to a luxury holiday site. We are thinking about a carefully planned, well researched, life-enhancing encounter with other countries. Done properly, an extended period of travel can have a positive impact on your life. It can change both your view of the world and the trajectory of your career. Knowing the world and understanding the limits of your ability to adapt to the complexities of humanity can be pivotal to your future.

For many young adults and their parents, the idea of spending a year abroad is a positive way to bridge the gap between school and adulthood and the life of work. Young Australians and New Zealanders often build the "gap year" into their transition to adulthood. European youth travel extensively within the continent, aided by low prices for air and rail travel. Well-to-do Asian youth — particularly from Japan, Hong Kong, and the wealthy enclaves in China — show up on youth trips, camps, and other adventure activities in countries around the world.

By contrast, the custom of postponing the leap into post-secondary education or work — of going outside the country to discover more about the world — is not well established in Canada. With few exceptions, young Canadians stay close to home. They have usually travelled only on standard, risk-free trips to Disney World, Hawaii, England, or Niagara Falls.

Canadians do not typically visit much of their own country, let alone travel to Zambia, Indonesia, or Bangladesh. Young Canadians often go into their adulthood having visited very few places and knowing very little about the world beyond what they learned in school — which, we can assure you, is not very much.

For a large number of Canadian youth, there is no great need to move forward with their studies, to sprint into the world of work — although, of course, some young people are forced by family and financial circumstances to get on with adult life as quickly as possible. If you can manage it, you should consider spending a significant period of time — four months to a year — travelling inside or outside Canada.

Put aside your travel paranoia, shift out of your comfort zone, and give careful thought to how you might explore a world that you perhaps don't know very well. There is a complex and exciting world to discover. The so-called "gap year" is a simple concept: you save up the funds to travel, buy an inexpensive ticket, decide where you are going to go (often with friends), and head off on a grand adventure. You will, if you plan your extended travel properly, learn a great deal about yourself and your place within the world as a whole.

Aussies and Kiwis, living in countries that have far greater loyalty to British traditions than Canada does, have colonial memories that lead them to travel to the "mother country," restoring family and cultural connections to the British Isles. Canadians, with so many different nations of origin, have no such common destination — although a sizeable number of anglophiles do make the transatlantic crossing. Travel farther afield. A visit to India will demonstrate the power of one of the world's most dynamic and complex societies. Travelling across Europe will fill you with a sense of historical and cultural wonder. Walking through the streets of the intense and rich city-state of Singapore will alert you to the potential of Asia. Travelling from the mega-city of New York through the plains of Oklahoma to the sprawling energy of Los Angeles will remind you of the power, possibilities, and crises of the contemporary United States. Driving from Cape Town to Johannesburg will reveal the comparative wealth and grinding poverty of South Africa. A few days in Moscow and St. Petersburg will demonstrate the combination of imperial majesty, Stalinist oppression, capitalist excess, and post-Communist decay that makes Russia so fascinating. Travel the world. Know the world. Discover yourself.

PAY FOR YOUR YEAR OF DISCOVERY YOURSELF

Maybe it is because we have nine children between us, making us cheap in the extreme, but we are not fans of free rides. If you are thinking of a year of travelling — and we sincerely hope that you will give this very serious thought — then start saving as early as possible. Many travellers work from the end of school into the early or late fall, then leave for eight months or so, giving them the option of starting school the following September. If you are frugal and really want to travel, you can save a fair bit of money during this period of time. There are many ways to add to your savings: high school graduation gifts from parents and grandparents, saved Christmas cash, money set aside from part-time work during high school. Parental support is always a possibility for well-to-do families, but we would not recommend that parents pay all or a large part of the cost.

It's not as cheap as it was fifty years ago, when one of us went across *Europe on Five Dollars a Day*, to cite the title of the popular book — but it still can be done at reasonable cost. Young adults who plan for their travels, pay all or a substantial portion of the costs involved, and spend frugally while on the road will get far more out of their experience that those who are simply given the whole thing as a present. There are many benefits from this approach, including the early experience with financial planning, the careful budgeting during the last stages of high school, attention to detail (such as who pays for the inoculations, which are generally not covered by health insurance), forward-looking preparation, and the delayed gratification that this entails — the satisfaction associated with taking responsibility for a big undertaking, the freedom that comes from paying for a major initiative oneself (making it harder for parents to direct the travel schedule), learning about foreign currencies and currency fluctuations, and the money management necessary to stretch the funds for the whole trip.

It's also a good idea to build work into your travel plans. By working along the route, a young traveller can easily double or triple the amount of time on the road, and pick up some experience along the way. There are useful working-visa programs for young workers in Australia, New Zealand, and the United Kingdom. These working visas are easy to get, flexible, and let you prolong your stay by working, generally in an unskilled job. It is a measure of the limited demand for these working visas among Canadians that the United Kingdom provides only 5,500 spaces for Canadians but 10,000 for New Zealanders and 35,000 for Australians. There are many opportunities for English-speaking au pairs and nannies across Europe and Asia — many young women (and not just young women) capitalize on such opportunities and use a few months' work to extend their travel time.

Work and save before you go, and then find occasional work during your travels. Convert a month-long visit to Europe into a year-long adventure around the world. As much as you possibly can, pay for the trip yourself. Convert your first major experience after high school into a declaration of independence. Travelling the world on someone else's dime is an extension of adolescence — fun but without the maturity, responsibility, and freedom to make your own choices. You are a high school graduate. You are about to make huge life choices that will frame your adulthood. You can start by taking full responsibility for financing what could and should be both a grand adventure and the launch of adulthood.

BE ADVENTUROUS, BUT BE CAREFUL

The worst thing that you can do with your travel time is to gather together with some high school friends, settle on an itinerary by consensus, and then head out together in a prolonged extension of a high school field trip. You may have one good friend who shares your interests and wants to explore, but making the journey into a group exercise is not the best way to go.

There is no fixed plan or direction for your travels. Some will head to the United Kingdom and Europe — expensive, familiar, easy to get around, and rich with history and culture. Many, fleeing Canadian winters, will target Australia and New Zealand — two great countries that have the advantage of being cheaper than Europe (but not much), with better work opportunities, great weather, and some of the most diverse and beautiful scenery in the world. We are all for these but, as we have already indicated, we favour a journey that takes you off the familiar and easy path.

Avoid the danger zones. One important sign of maturity — and one way of stopping your parents from having a fit — is to deliberately avoid conflict regions. If you want a test of this, go to the library and take out a copy of Robert Young Pelton's *The World's Most Dangerous Places*. Leave it sitting on the living room table. Watch your mother age before your eyes. Expect to be taken for a serious walk by your father. There are so many wonderful and fascinating places to visit that you do not need to put yourself at risk. If you want to go to the Middle East, pick Turkey, Qatar, and the United Arab Emirates, not Saudi Arabia, Iraq, or Iran. Stay away from Kashmir on the India-Pakistan border, but do seek out the major cities in India.

Think about the world's greatest cities — London, Paris, Stockholm, Istanbul, Copenhagen, Sydney, Auckland, Hong Kong, Singapore, New York, and, yes, Montreal and Vancouver, two of the greatest urban places on the planet. Don't avoid the poorer cities: there are some — São Paulo, Rio de Janeiro, and Buenos Aires are good examples — that are impressive, modern cities with huge slums connected with them.

Take in some of the world's greatest human-made wonders, like the Great Wall of China, the Hermitage in St. Petersburg, the Eiffel Tower, the pyramids, the Japanese *Shinkansen* (bullet train), the Acropolis in Athens, the Colosseum in Rome, Stonehenge in England, and the Old City of Jerusalem. Find a hundred places you have never heard of and never anticipated, for in these unexpected discoveries lie the real mysteries of humanity.

DO A REALITY CHECK

But here is one of those periodic tests that we inflict on you. If the lists above do not make you curious, if you did not grab an atlas or travel book or go online to check some of them out, you have just revealed a great deal about yourself. The places above — and thousands more — are wonderful. Visiting them should make your heart soar (or plunge, depending on your reaction to some of the hardships). If you were unmoved, if the prospect of exploring the world simply left you cold, you are not a bad or terrible person, but you are likely to remain place-bound for much of your life, and your world will be limited accordingly.

But you have just learned an important lesson: you like the familiar, you like being comfortable, you are not adventurous (at least not yet), and the idea of travelling does not inspire you. Incidentally, and this is a crucial point, you may not be ready for university either — if you cannot be inspired by the prospect of exploring the world in a physical way, it is unlikely that exploring it mentally through literature, history, geography, sociology, politics, or any other field will appeal much to you.

CONNECT WITH ASIA

As you plan your trip, make sure that you include Asia in your travels. For a growing number of young Canadians, the continent is at least somewhat familiar because it's part of their family's history. The large numbers of young Indo-Canadians, Chinese Canadians, Pakistani Canadians, Vietnamese Canadians, and other Asian Canadians have obvious reasons for connecting with Asia.

For Canadians whose cultural and ethnic origins are in Europe, North America, South America, or Africa, Asia is often remote and mysterious, if not threatening. Asia is the land of the Chinese economic juggernaut, the broiling Indian cities, South Korean technology, Japan's anime, Pakistan's political instability, Vietnam's wartime legacy, and thousands of other things. It is hot, except where it is cold, densely crowded except where there are large stretches of almost open land, industrially competitive save for where hundreds of millions subsist on hard-scrabble farming, democratic where it is not run by dictators and one-party states. Asia is a land of a million contradictions, the source of much of the world's economic anxiety and hope for future prosperity.

As you prepare for a twenty-first-century life, you have to come to terms with Asia. The West has seen the emergence of the region as an economic powerhouse, with two of the three largest economies in the world, as a threatening development. In fact, Asia's economic power is a return to form. Before the onset of industrialization in the late eighteenth century,

China was the world's largest economy and Asia was globally prominent. Colonialism, wars, Communism, and American expansionism allowed the West to overtake Asia and even to subjugate much of it. No longer. The ascendency of Asia will be perhaps the most important phenomenon of the twenty-first century.

While parts of Asia are no-go zones — stay away from Burma, many parts of Pakistan, and any part of the continent experiencing civil unrest or insurrection — most of it is safe for you. The government of Canada's Foreign Affairs website provides excellent advice for anyone thinking of travelling in the region. Common sense prevails. Get caught with drugs in Singapore or Thailand and you won't be home any time soon, if ever. Engage in anti-government protests in China and don't be surprised if the authorities are seriously unimpressed. For a young North American woman, wandering into the bar culture in parts of Japan can bring serious problems.

A well-planned trip should include a substantial amount of time in Japan (the safest and most accessible country in Asia), China (and don't stay in the big cities the whole time), Hong Kong, Singapore, and South Korea. Vietnam is well worth a visit as it is a potential economic power-house, still recovering from both the long war with the United States and the decades-long boycott that followed. Laos and Cambodia are interesting but travel is more difficult. Indonesia has some very accessible places — Bali is a major tourist destination and Jakarta is a modern city — but many of the hundreds of islands that make up the country are difficult to reach and somewhat uncomfortable for travellers. Thailand is a diverse country and is well worth the trip — but the parts that attract young people are best known for wild partying. Follow the cultural circuits in the country and the rewards are significant.

Many travellers have difficulty with South Asia — Bangladesh, India, Sri Lanka, and Pakistan — but the region is more accommodating than most expect. There are serious extremes of wealth and poverty, and the misery in some of the major urban slums and poor rural areas can be very upsetting to well-off Canadians. Still, this region is experiencing an interesting combination of rapid population increase and economic growth, political instability and democratization, religious tension and multicultural collaboration, technological innovation and ancient class systems. We would put Asia this way: you have to see it to believe it. Besides, many of the patterns of your life, for good and bad, are going to be set in Asia. Get used to it and get to know it.

HAVE FUN WITH YOUR PLANNING

If you are keen, do not just follow our lead. Explore — online and in books — and discover the parts of the world that interest you. You'll love some of the places you go and dislike others. In the process, you'll create a personal mental map of your world, and figure out your own place within it.

With these warnings in mind, have fun with your planning. The preparations can be enjoyable and even exciting. Here are some things to look for:

- **Multi-stop around the world tickets!** One of the best travel deals in the world. For about $3,500, you can go all the way around the world, provided you keep going in one direction.

- **International Hostelling Association memberships.** This is another one of the best travel deals in the world. Youth hostels are typically well situated, inexpensive, safe, and well managed. Staying at an accredited centre carries many benefits in terms of accessibility, reservations, local knowledge, Internet facilities, and the like.

- **Tour companies specializing in trips for young adults.** There are many of these around, the Kiwi experience being one of the best for young people — light on the luxury, heavy on the camaraderie and fun. These are typically inexpensive, enjoyable, and well-organized tours that combine the best of sight-seeing with opportunities targeted at young adults.

- **Ways to connect travelling and volunteer activities.** Habitat for Humanity, for example, arranges tours in association with many of their building projects.

- **Needles.** Go to the local travel medicine centre, give them a list of all of the countries you will be visiting, and roll up your sleeve! Get all of the needles you require, especially those for diseases like dengue fever, hepatitis, malaria, and yellow fever. Trust the specialists. They know what you need and they are more cautious than you are. We can assure you of this. You do not want to get sick with a tropical or strange illness in a country without a proper health care system. If you are one of the people who think that vaccination is a Big Pharma plot, stay home, unless you have a death wish.

- **Good travel insurance.** The best agencies offer excellent local support in most countries and move quickly to get you into top-quality hospitals (which are very different than those provided to the local population). Do not skimp on the insurance arrangements.

- **Local cellphone service.** Coverage is excellent in many counties. Rural Vietnam is typically better and cheaper than many places in rural Canada, for example. The problem comes with the roaming charges for your Canadian telephone service. In most countries, it is much — as in a huge amount — cheaper to buy local pay-as-you-go service than to pay your Canadian wireless service provider. Most international airports have cheap and reliable wireless sales counters.

- **Travel guides and books.** You can get quite a bit out of a decent travel book — *Lonely Planet* and *Rough* guides are excellent — and more people learn about the history, culture, and politics of foreign lands from these guides than from traditional sources. We strongly urge you to read serious books of history, politics, society, or current affairs before you head into a new country or while you are there. You will get much more out of your travels than if you try to pick up background and information on the fly. With Kobo, Kindle, or iPad readers, you can pack a hundred books with less weight than a single hardcover book.

BE PREPARED FOR A LIFE-CHANGING EXPERIENCE

Will travelling make you a better student or employee? It's hard to say for sure. Travel — and we are talking here about four to twelve months, not a quick trip to Cuba to lie on the beach — will certainly make you a more interesting person. It will broaden your horizons, make you more self-reliant, build your confidence and independence, introduce you to the importance of cross-cultural understanding, and expose you to both the richness and the poverty of the world. The maturity level of young people who have ventured far from home, making their way with of the care and attention to detail across many countries, is often profoundly different from that average high school graduate.

When you are on the road, you will confront a hundred significant choices a day. Lie on the beach or visit a world-famous museum? Share pizza with friends from the hostel or spend a very risky evening with rowdier folks you met at the bar? Jump on a bus heading into remote mountain villages or stay in the safety of a familiar major city? Change your schedule so you can help stomp the grapes in a winery in Spain or stick to the plan that you set out six months earlier when you had no sense of the possibilities. You will make judgments about new friends and travel companions. You will negotiate with your partner or a group about issues large and small. You will adjust to new foods, accommodate different social and religious conventions, and learn to operate in a wide variety of political, legal, and economic environments. You will cope with crises, some of them potentially serious, and learn to negotiate, navigate, and otherwise fend for yourself in very complex settings.

We do not want to oversell the economic and career value of a year of travel. Very few employers are going to hire you as a vice-president on the basis of the two months you spent climbing and hiking in Nepal or working at a winery in New Zealand. The right kind of travel — have we warned you about avoiding the debauchery zones in Thailand or the pot cafés in Amsterdam? — will draw the attention of admissions officers and human resource recruiters, if only because it makes you more interesting than your competitors who have not wandered very far from Mississauga, Surrey, or Sherwood Park. As well, you will likely be much more interested in the world and could develop a life-long fascination with the people, economies, and politics of the places that you visited.

What are you searching for? The answer is simple: yourself and your future. To find either of these, you will do well to embrace the challenge of travel, move away from where you are comfortable, and see just how far you can push yourself. There is great pleasure to be found in discovering yourself and learning about far-off places. Do this with joy, careful planning, strict money management, and a desire to become a true citizen of the world.

CHAPTER EIGHT

ENTREPRENEURSHIP: WHY WAIT TO BE YOUR OWN BOSS?

LOOK INTO ENTREPRENEURSHIP AS A CAREER

There is a great deal of talk in Canada these days about the "skills gap," the "knowledge economy," and the value of a post-secondary education. Canada has a more serious deficit, however — and there is perhaps the greatest opportunity for young people — in the field of entrepreneurship. Entrepreneurs are the people who start and run the businesses, not those who apply to work for them. And they are a breed apart. There aren't enough in this country, but perhaps you are one of them.

When people try to explain why the United States still has (for the moment at least) the world's largest economy, they usually think first of the country's remarkable risk-taking environment (unless they're on the political left, in which case they give other reasons: the legacy of slavery, capitalist exploitation, and the like). Gambling is in America's blood, right down to bankruptcy laws that enable people to write a bad debt experience off their books, to bounce back from financial crisis, and to plunge boldly back into the world of business creation. The country is crazy about its financial high-rollers. How else can the attention paid to a high-stakes gambler and loudmouth self-promoter like Donald Trump be explained, when serious and far more important people like Yo-Yo Ma, Noam Chomsky, Daniel Boorstin, and David Frum are little known outside limited circles? There are other countries with a finely tuned entrepreneurial drive — Israel is a world leader, and places like Japan, South Korea, Taiwan, and Singapore have well-developed business development cultures that drive their economies. But no one really does business quite like the Americans.

Canada, in contrast, is a slow mover on the entrepreneurial front. We have our great entrepreneurs — people like Seymour Schulich, Heather Reisman (ever visited a Chapters/Indigo store?), Jim Pattison (Mr. Everything in B.C.), Tom Jenkins (Open Text), the Sobey, McCain, and Irving families in the Maritimes, Peter Nygard, and hundreds of others who have done amazing work in their home regions. Few people outside the Yukon know of the remarkable business and community-building activities of Rolf Hougen. Especially impressive is Chief Robert Louie's work with the Osoyoos First Nation in B.C.

In typical Canadian fashion, however, we often rush to point out the entrepreneurs who fall on their faces — the founders of one-time high technology superstar firms such as JDS Uniphase, Nortel, and now Research In Motion/

> **STOP RIGHT HERE ...**
>
> Do you recognize all or any of these names? Are you curious about them? Remember the curiosity test; you can look them all up.

BlackBerry (although you should keep your eyes on Mike Lazaridis's new push into quantum computing). It is true that many of our richest Canadians inherited their money (the Thomsons, Irvings, and Westons), but many others made their fortunes in land development or in the fast-growing energy sector in western Canada.

For some reason, perhaps because it seems un-Canadian, young people don't know much about the career and life opportunities of entrepreneurship. There are a number of organizations aimed at young entrepreneurs: the Canadian Junior Chamber of Commerce, Young Women in Business, the Canadian Youth Business Foundation (and their FuEL Awards initiative), and 4-H Canada (for the agriculturally minded). The Business Development Bank of Canada's Young Entrepreneur Award program supports young business people, and many schools, colleges, and universities now offer programs specifically to train people for entrepreneurship. Shad Valley, one of the most impressive youth development programs anywhere, focuses on building entrepreneurial expertise and determination. Make sure you look at Impact, an excellent youth-run program for university-level entrepreneurs. Young people who are intrigued by the prospects and opportunities associated with running a business should check out these and other organizations. But unfortunately, too few young Canadians give much thought to entrepreneurship, instead spending a great deal of time and energy figuring how they can prepare themselves to work for someone else.

EXAMINE YOURSELF: ARE YOU A BORN ENTREPRENEUR?

University professors have intense debates about whether or not entrepreneurship can be taught. It does seem odd that these people, secure in their government-supported positions, would be teaching young people how to take risks, make business-threatening decisions, and deal with commercial reality. The consensus, however, appears to be that people can be taught to understand entrepreneurship. And — if they have the basic skills and mindset — they also can be taught how to capitalize on their abilities and convert motivation, commercial ideas, and energy into a successful business. Put a different way, a lack of guidance and preparation can make the path to successful entrepreneurship even tougher than it already is.

But maybe you are one of those who have natural entrepreneurial skills in their DNA. You are the one who is always looking for an opportunity to make money, who organized the spring break skiing trip and made a nice profit from it, who rebuilds cars and sells them for a 40 percent return on the initial investment, who took the sleepy little concession stand run by the student council and turned it into a big money-spinner, who started tweaking some computer programs in high school and ended up creating three apps that are now hosted on the Apple site. A born entrepreneur is not just the smooth-talking used-car salesperson type, although some of you out there are like that as well.

The really transformative entrepreneurs do not just sell, speculate, or develop (all fine things), but they also create. And they not only create new businesses, but also new products and even entire commercial sectors. The late Steve Jobs, Bill Gates, Mike Lazaradis, Arlene Dickinson, and Heather Reisman are great examples. Another example is Mark Zuckerberg, founder of Facebook, who took some basic computer code and converted it into a $100 billion enterprise.

Young millionaires flourished during the dot-com boom in the late 1990s — and some of them, the true entrepreneurs, survived the bust. They took their digital earnings and invested them in new companies and new ventures. They built on their initial technological innovation, used the money to invest in other businesses, and continued on in a life of commercial creativity. They now form the foundation of the high technology industry in Canada and the

> READ THE RECENT BIOGRAPHY OF STEVE JOBS ...
>
> Are you anything like him?

United States, although they are no longer the geeks and hackers of earlier days. Most importantly, these high-tech business people made entrepreneurship acceptable and even exciting, in a way that business development, auto-parts manufacturing, and construction never did. It turned out that the most successful ones — Gates and Jobs being the best examples — were far more than techies who got lucky on the digital bubble; instead, they were savvy, high-risk entrepreneurs sniffing out profit and opportunity by staying just ahead of the global technological curve.

CONSIDER SOME BASIC QUESTIONS

The starting point is important. Some people are meant to be entrepreneurs, but most are not. True entrepreneurial spirit — by which we mean the ability and drive to create, not simply the capacity to turn a profit — is extremely rare. When the two elements merge — entrepreneurial spirit and core business ability — the results can be spectacular, as people like Tom Jenkins (chief strategy officer of OpenText, Canada's largest software company) and Mike Lazaradis demonstrate.

At this stage in your life, you can consider some basic questions:

- Do I like making money?

- Do I enjoy taking risks?

- Am I really, seriously, over-the-top, dedicated, and hard-working?

- Am I willing to "eat what I kill," or live off of what I earn from business?

- Do I learn quickly, from both life experience and organized education, so that I can get the core skills I need to succeed?

- Do I insist on being my own boss?

If you can answer these questions with a resounding "yes," then you should seriously consider starting your own business, during or after high school, or after university or college.

Now consider a second set of questions:

- Do I like to invent or create things?

- Do I like figuring out how things work — or do not work?

- Do I find myself a little out of sync with my classmates, seeing the world somewhat differently than others?

- Do I think I am right most of the time — and am I willing to work hard to prove it?

If you answer the second set with a strong affirmative, then you are a creative thinker, a "do-er" with real imagination and the capacity to anticipate change. This might make you an artist, a writer, a politician, or the leader of a social movement.

Now here's the trick. If you answered yes to both sets of questions — one about your drive to make a profit and the second about your imaginative side — you might be on the path to being a true entrepreneur. If you think that this defines you, don't neglect this aspect of your personality. The true entrepreneurs are the innovators who sustain and improve prosperity, who make their families, communities, and country better. It is a real gift to be truly business-minded. It is wonderful to be intelligent and creative. It is extremely rare to be all those things. For these true entrepreneurs, the future can be a bonanza. And our country could use a lot more people like them.

LEARN FROM LIFE, NOT SCHOOL

High school does not create entrepreneurs, nor, with some exceptions, does university or college. Most teachers, civil-servant-like and unionized, don't have the skills to teach entrepreneurship. If they did, they wouldn't be teachers. They might be friendly to the local business people, and might even create some policy space for them in the school. But they are not going to do very much to turn students into entrepreneurs. Classes on business focus on the basics of law, policy, and bookkeeping — not on the blood and guts of starting, building, losing, and selling a start-up business.

Universities and colleges have stepped into the game, offering all manner of courses, programs, targeted residences for young entrepreneurs, extra-curricular activities, awards, clubs, and other related initiatives. Boot camps, like the University of Toronto's offering for thirty-two top young entrepreneurs that works outside the conventional classroom to help young creative people convert ideas into businesses, are all the rage. Much later on, when you have at least one degree under your belt, you can think about the Master of Business Entrepreneurship and Technology program at the Conrad Centre at the University of Waterloo — an unconventional program that turns traditional business education inside out and lights a spark under budding business developers. But you are not there yet.

At this point, you are pretty much on your own. Unless you have a favourite teacher with an entrepreneurial bent (there are a few), a family friend who serves as your mentor, or entrepreneurship running deep in the family, there will not be a lot of help for you. Entrepreneurs stick out from the crowd — there will not be many classmates who understand what motivates you or who share your passion for business or creativity. You should seek out people who think as you do. Real entrepreneurs in the community — the Big Men and Women about Town — are probably your best bet as mentors. These successful folks are often among the very best supporters of young entrepreneurs and can be a huge help in the future. They are often surprisingly accessible. They knew what it took to launch their careers, and are often on the lookout for bright, talented young entrepreneurs.

START SMALL — AND YOUNG

While there are many examples of successful entrepreneurs who came to private business later in life, most entrepreneurs seem to have a lifetime fascination with the field. The central characteristic of young business leaders is that they are willing to work hard to get rich. These days we have almost lost one of the most important points of entry for such people. Not so long ago, when almost every house in town had the paper delivered, pre-teen boys and girls by the thousands walked Canadian streets each morning, delivering the daily paper. The job of a paper carrier involved running a mini-business: selling subscriptions, delivering the paper (sub-contracting when away on holiday), collecting money, keeping the books, dealing with deadbeat subscribers, and, eventually, pocketing the profits. This is almost gone now. Adults deliver most newspapers — kids deliver the free flyers, which is not at all business-like — and there are so few subscribers that many of those delivering papers drive from one to the next. The really difficult and character-building parts — which involved collecting money, recording income, and paying bills — have all been replaced by online billing and payment systems. There were other options: shovelling snow, mowing lawns, running a juice stand in the summer, and so on, and some of these are still around.

The main point is simple. Even pre-teens could get a start in business. You are probably all puzzled by this, because most of these junior entrepreneurial opportunities have evaporated over the last twenty years. This does not mean that there are no jobs for young people — thousands of people work in family businesses or local stores, restaurants, and service outlets. And there are still babies to be sat — current rate where we live is upwards of five dollars an hour. But that's not entrepreneurial; it's more like getting paid for doing chores.

We have seen a slow and steady decline in tiny owner-operated businesses, the kind that taught hard lessons about commerce — getting even well-to-do adults to pay their newspaper subscriptions on time was often challenging. Think of the shifts that have occurred. New Canadian adults have taken many of the jobs formerly done by young people. Online billing and payment systems have eliminated the need to collect payments personally. Parents are much easier on their children and often provide them with an allowance that covers more than they could earn through operating a small business. Few young people go door to door to solicit snow-shovelling or lawn-mowing business — and the ones who do are often college-aged or new Canadians, and only rarely teenagers.

So getting experience in entrepreneurship is a little harder than in the past, but is far from impossible. Starting young is essential, in business as in athletics, music, writing, or any other worthwhile endeavour. Malcolm Gladwell's observation that achieving excellence and pre-eminence requires some 10,000 hours of practice holds for business as for anything else. If you want to hone the skills of a high-achieving business person, you have to practise, learn, practise, and, when you are feel you are almost there, start practising again and again.

This is easy to understand in the context of hockey, music, or painting. Very few people become right-wingers on the Montreal Canadiens without countless hours of practice. The first violinist in the Edmonton Symphony Orchestra might have been a child prodigy, but that skill was then developed, sharpened, and improved through years of practice. We don't think about marketing, human resource management, investing, bookkeeping, product development, supply chain operations and logistics, innovation, and risk-taking in the same terms, but becoming a successful business person or commercial leader is no different. You have to work at it.

You can follow the standard pattern in Canada — coast through high school and then head to college or university for a diploma or degree in business. Then, armed with a college or university credential, you will do what most young Canadians do, which is search for a job with a decent employer. Postponing your plans to become an entrepreneur makes sense in one regard. In today's business environment, you will likely need advanced technical or professional skills. Including some advanced education in your development is a wise idea. But you need to develop the basic habits and mindset early. If you wait till your mid-twenties to begin, your dream of starting your own company, launching a new project, or becoming a true entrepreneur will almost certainly never be realized.

Start now. Hit it hard. Find a business opportunity. Do your research. Plan carefully and thoughtfully and then move on it. You might start very small, mowing lawns for the neighbours, washing cars, or providing some other basic service. Be good at it. Deliver a top-quality service or product, and do it with full attention to your customers and your business. Hire someone to help you. Set up proper books. Figure out the licences and regulations. Take the idea of launching a business very seriously; give it the same amount of attention you might later spend launching a college, polytech, or university career.

The learning benefit of a year or two spent running a small business is immense. You will be laying the groundwork for later ventures into commerce, while you are also going to discover whether you thrive — or shrivel — under the pressures of running a proper business. Some young entrepreneurs take a big leap, buying into a more sizeable business and running the company while continuing their studies. (If you can stomach an old Tom Cruise movie — and this one is actually pretty good — watch *Risky Business*. The business model is lucrative but hard to sell to your parents — he turns the family home into a brothel when his folks are away. But, as he soon discovers, there is form and structure to every successful business.) Our point is simple. Entrepreneurship is both a skill and a passion. You have to develop the skill and feed the passion. You can and should start young and start small.

DON'T JUMP WITHOUT PREPARATION ...

It takes real guts to take the first step, to launch into business. If you cannot bring yourself to jump, or at least to take a significant step, you will have learned a great lesson about yourself.

But, if you are going to jump, do your homework first. Plan carefully, with close attention to the details:

- Is the idea sound?

- Do you have the money?

- Who is going to do the work?

- What is the market and audience?

- Do you need a business licence or any other approvals?

Review everything with a mentor, preferably a business person who has been down this path before. And with the work down and the planning well in hand, do it.

Venture nothing, gain nothing.

BE PREPARED TO TAKE RISKS — AND TO GO BACK TO SCHOOL

Business is about risk above all else. It involves taking a calculated gamble about commerce and personal choices. You are putting it all on the line — your money, your time, and your reputation. Once you hang out your shingle (putting out a sign to announce the start of a new business, typically in law or medicine — another reference that means nothing these days), your name and your business idea are open to the public. What you thought was a terrific idea — delivering cakes and cookies to children's birthday parties — could easily go down in flames. These days, the Internet makes it easier to hide your commercial experiment. Your attempt to make money by being the 694th iPhone application offering fart sounds could collapse in digital humiliation, but the odds are very good that few people will learn of your embarrassing experience. Remember, too, that most successful business people started and failed several times before they found their niche.

Being a young entrepreneur holds a great deal of promise. You will find out whether you like the field and whether you have the nerve, work ethic, and determination to succeed — and the brains to know when to shift gears, close down shop, move to another business idea, or adapt to changing circumstances. The chances are quite small that you will, as a teenager, find the business that will propel you through life. What you will find is whether entrepreneurship is for you, if not immediately then when you have prepared yourself better for the real challenges.

So, to encourage you, here are the top five lessons that we think you will gain from running a small business when you are young:

- **You will figure out if entrepreneurship is for you.** Most people will never be entrepreneurs. You need to find out whether you have what it takes, and whether you have the ideas and the creativity to look at the work around you and find a way to make money.

- **You will discover the strong connection between work ethic and personal outcomes.** If you work harder, you will likely make more money. Slack off as a small business owner and your income plummets. This is one of the most important life lessons.

- **You will find out if you have good business sense.** While there are many technical aspects to running a successful business, the key attributes are less formal. You will find out whether you have the instincts to identify opportunity, the strength to bargain hard, and the integrity to build a proper business.

- **You will discover your openness to risk.** Business is about taking calculated gambles on a daily basis. If life in a risk-filled environment is stressful and unnerving, you'd better plan on a different career.

- **You will quickly learn that ideas and work ethic are not enough on their own.** You will need technical and professional skills — keeping the books and paying taxes is essential. Being a smooth-talking, hard-working, amiable salesperson is not sufficient on its own.

Teenage businesses can bring in hundreds of dollars a month, enough for a lot of iTunes downloads and regular visits to the movieplex. Really successful ones — and there are hundreds of such young business people out there — can make thousands of dollars a year. With a little family financing, hard work, and some good luck you could have a solid business in operation.

But you may find out that this is not enough. One of the big discoveries for many budding business people is that they need additional skills — technical, professional, or commercial. Having money is much better than the alternative, but is often not sufficient on its own. For people wanting to make the most of their careers — and to push their business abilities to the maximum — commercial success often leads to college or university for the specialized training that is required for real success.

Don't be surprised, therefore, if you find out that your success as an entrepreneur leads you to an accelerated program of self-improvement and further discovery. Indeed, now that you've experienced that remarkable combination of risk, effort, intelligence, and commerce, you might well find that you are much more motivated to do well academically than those around you. After all, you've learned all about opportunity costs and are making significant sacrifices to be back in school — and you have your eye on a much bigger prize, particularly the wealth and freedom associated with being an independent business person.

REMEMBER THAT YOU'RE ALSO HELPING YOUR COUNTRY

It's not entirely about you, either. While entrepreneurship can lead you to an exciting and rewarding career, there are also vital nation-building elements to this kind of activity. We live in a globalized and highly competitive world. Canadians compete for business — and therefore for jobs, wealth, and stability — with entrepreneurs and innovators in countries around the world. Those places that win at the entrepreneurial game — and again we draw your attention to places like Israel, Taiwan, and Singapore that are doing particularly well right now in this regard — stand to prosper in the coming years. Canadians, in contrast, have fallen back on our natural resource wealth to sustain our very high standard of living.

It is instructive to consider the history of the Region of Waterloo in southern Ontario. The Kitchener-Waterloo-Cambridge area — Canada's Technology Triangle — has been a leader in innovation for many years. Time and again over the past decades, the Region of Waterloo reinvented itself, in keeping with the changes in the national and global economy. Twenty years ago, the automobile sector was riding high in the region. Starting about a decade ago, this industry took a battering from which it has not yet recovered. Even before Mike Lazardis and Jim Balsillie took Research In Motion from being a small paging company into the elite world of mobile Internet and messaging, local entrepreneurs and investors (many of whom made their money in land development) started to build a high technology economy. Waterloo is now known as Silicon Valley North — home to hundreds of start-up companies, angel investors, serial entrepreneurs, and one of the most mutually supportive business climates in the world. If you live nearby, look at Communitech (an impressive business development initiative), The Hub (an incubator for start-up operations), and the digital media campus in nearby Stratford.

There are some new groups developing across the country, in places as diverse as Fredericton (aided by some impressive leadership from local entrepreneurs Desh Deshpande and Gerry Pond), Montreal, Vancouver, Calgary, and Saskatoon. There are government and banking programs by the dozens, as Canadian governments and financial institutions seek to promote business development. But the country needs more. In particular, Canada requires many more young people to consider entrepreneurship as a career. For some, this means nothing more than gut-wrenching risk taking — a flyer on local real estate that might turn into a lucrative land development business. For others, years of advanced study in engineering, applied science (love that biotechnology, nanotechnology, and quantum computing stuff), and business are required to make a move into their highly technical sector. For all of these future business leaders and entrepreneurs, it requires a particular type of mind — one that is freed from the need to follow the well-trodden path to the human resources office or the employment centre, that finds risk energizing, that builds off of a formidable work commitment, and that has real staying power.

If Canada is to flourish in the twenty-first century, it urgently needs builders, thinkers, risk-takers, creators, and innovators. It needs the young people with the verve and enthusiasm to tackle the challenges and complexities of the global economy. These people — and perhaps you are one of them — have the ideas or business drive to create new companies and produce the thousands of jobs that the country requires to sustain its enviable standard of living. We do not do particularly well in this regard at present, in part because we spend so much time and effort preparing young people to work for others. We are a nation of employees, not investors, of middle managers and civil servants rather than entrepreneurs.

You will know if you have what it takes in terms of drive, energy, and determination. If you don't, that's okay too — we don't either, and we've had happy and productive lives. Business is not for the faint-hearted, and entrepreneurship is not for the weak. Nor, interestingly, is it restricted to the smartest or those with the best grades (one of the standing jokes about universities is that they are where A students teach B students so that they can work for C students). Entrepreneurship is more about mindset and work

CANADA NEEDS THOUSANDS MORE KUMAL GUPTAS

Kumal Gupta is a former University of Waterloo student, one of the founders of the Impact program for young entrepreneurs, and the CEO of Polar Mobile, a company that helps content producers move their information onto mobile devices. Kumal started Polar Mobile when he was an undergraduate — a time, by his own admission, when he was often too busy with his business activities to devote much time to his studies as an engineer (although he did graduate).

With the persistence of the true entrepreneur, and while still in his early twenties, he wormed his way into some of the leading information companies in North America and persuaded them to try his media product. If you read *Elle*, *Hockey News*, *Wired*, the *Toronto Star*, or any of some four hundred other publications on your mobile device, you are probably using a Polar Mobile product.

Perhaps most importantly, and a time when many budding entrepreneurs have taken their ideas and talents to the often more lucrative (and warmer) environments in the United States, Kumal and his company have stayed in Canada, using this country as a base to serve customers in a dozen nations.

ethic than it is about intellectual capacity and high school grades. If you have it, or if you think you have, immerse yourself in the sector. Hang out with those motivated by business. Figure out where opportunities and your interests collide. A successful young entrepreneur in Ontario in recent years found his opportunity in selling male cosmetics online, identifying an unfilled market niche and profiting from it. Explore and try it out. The country's future might well rest on your success. And if you do really well, you can make a point of hiring some of the brainiacs from high school to work for you.

CHAPTER NINE

GIVE WORK A CHANCE

GET A JOB

The University of Waterloo has a nationally famous co-op program that mixes work with study. You would think that people coming into such a program would know something about the world of work. But surprisingly, about a quarter of them have never held any kind of job before coming to university. This seems completely illogical. The co-operative education program is designed to produce career-ready graduates, fired up, motivated, and primed for the workforce. And yet a quarter of the students entering a program that focuses on practical and applied work come to it without ever having worked.

The reason for this seems to be that young Canadians have busy lives these days, but these lives do not always involve working for money. School takes up considerable amount of time. Many of the best students are heavily involved in extra-curricular activities — competitive sports, student government, volunteer groups, music, or drama. Add to this the inevitable summer camp, family travel, socializing, video games, and what have you, and there may be little time left for employment.

Others of you are, in fact, working. You sell tickets at the movie theatre, hand out the fries and donuts at the fast-food restaurants, work the counter at the local store, and otherwise serve in the army of part-time, low-wage workers that keep the Canadian service economy going. Fewer of you have *good* summer jobs, in part because desperate university students and recent graduates are grabbing most of the decent positions. And even the old entry-level posts in the retail stores and restaurants are going to adults (many of them new Canadians) and your new competition — senior citizens looking to supplement their incomes. For those of you in low-income families, these jobs are absolutely crucial. They allow you to save for college or university or (especially for new Canadians) supplement the family income.

Here's the point: you don't work because you love the smell of stale French fry oil or because staying up past midnight to vacuum spilled popcorn off a theatre floor feeds your love of the arts. You work because you want to and have to — and in doing so are developing attitudes toward life and responsibility that will serve you well in the years to come.

If you aren't poor, you work because you want the extras. Your parents won't cough up for the latest Samsung Galaxy, they balk at paying for your girlfriend's ticket to the movies, they make you cover the cost of insurance and gas for your car, or they refuse to buy the beer (or substance *du jour*) for your weekend parties. (You won't be surprised to learn that we're on your parents' side, most of the time.)

But there's a benefit to work that goes beyond getting money for fun. First, you learn the discipline of the workplace — showing up on time, being responsible, doing your job well, responding to criticism, taking direction, and the like. Second, you learn the direct relationship between work effort and the stuff money buys. Want the new cellphone that costs $750? Even the most math-challenged can figure out that at a job that pays $10 an hour (minus taxes, some benefits, the costs of getting to and from work, and related expenses), it will take close to a hundred hours of work to pay for it. That's a lot of fries served. And what good is the phone without a monthly data plan? Welcome to the world of McJobs.

Despite the various good reasons for working, it is parents who, in a growing number of middle-income and wealthy families, provide a first line of defence against the horrors of paid work. After all, if one of Mom and Dad's goals is to protect you from a blue-collar, working-class life, they're hardly going to applaud your decision to clean toilets at the local hotel, cut grass for the city, do telephone solicitation, or deliver pizzas.

So here you are, a few weeks or months away from graduation. You still don't know what you want to do. Your parents, teachers, and guidance counsellors keep yammering away about preparing yourself for the world of work, picking a career, studying for a profession, or otherwise finding a way to pay your way through life. But at a basic level, you have only a theoretical idea of what they are talking about. What is this work stuff?

What's it like to work from nine to five, or two weeks on/two off on the night shift, or as a casual employee? And what are offices like? Factories? Construction sites? Retail warehouses? Telemarketing operations? You have to make a choice, but on what basis? A few days of job shadowing? Presentations at career day? A little online research? Get real. None of this is worth a bucket of warm spit, to quote an American politician of an earlier day (except he didn't say "spit"). Here's a radical thought: get a job!

BUY SOME TIME

There's no rush to get to university, a polytechnic, or college. If you aren't yet convinced that post-secondary education is right for you — at least not at this moment — then don't go. We've argued earlier that there are other choices — travel or volunteering, for example — that you should consider very seriously. But why not consider the world of work? In many parts of the country, there are reasonably good short-term jobs available for bright, hard-working young people. We are not talking here about great careers necessarily, but rather about experience-enhancing opportunities to test yourself and to try out the working life.

Consider it an exercise in buying yourself some time. Get a job and set a financial goal or purpose (save money for a trip, post-secondary education, a car, a place of your own, whatever). Don't just wander aimlessly into the workforce. Those who do will often pop their heads up twenty years on and discover that they're in the same place. Plan your entry into the job market with the same kind of energy and thought you might otherwise give to going to college or university. Done properly, spending a year or two in the workforce could well prove to be precisely the right thing for you to do. And even if you wander aimlessly into a low-end job, it will be a learning experience, as long as you don't get stuck in it.

For young people who have never held a regular, long-term job, employment is as much foreign territory as the favelas of São Paulo. There are wonderful and difficult people in almost equal measure. There are great jobs and terrible jobs. Try inseminating cows (with a gizmo, not — um — you know what we mean) if you want a rough introduction to the realities of life. If that is not your style, get a job in a slaughterhouse or swab toilets in a nightclub. You could also work with mentally challenged adults (one of life's most surprisingly rewarding opportunities), assist with the production of live theatre, work backstage at a concert hall or for a Canadian Football League team. Work can be — and almost always is — challenging, fun, awful, hard, disappointing, and fulfilling, sometimes all at the same time.

The message here is simple. Try out work right out of high school. You will almost certainly discover that the kind of job you get is hard, doesn't bring in much money, and doesn't seem to have much of a future. It can also be a great incentive to go back to school.

APPROACH YOUR FIRST JOB AS A LEARNING EXPERIENCE

Of course, not everyone who leaves high school for the workforce ends up in a low-income, dead-end job, destined for a life with few prospects for happiness or a high income. Stephen is one of these exceptions. He is a super bright lad, truly gifted with computers. Early on, while still in high school, he presented himself to one of the leading technology entrepreneurs in the country and said he wanted a job. He had nothing to sell. So he did some voluntary work, and convinced the company to take him on. With nothing more than a high school diploma, he became a valuable member of the company. Several years later, he was earning a big salary — and attending university part-time at the insistence of his employer, reinforcing his self-taught skills with some brain-enhancing learning. Stephen shows that great things can result from leaping feet first into the workforce. But there are only a handful of Stephens out there.

If you are one of them, you might find your niche in life as fast in the world of work as in university, or faster. Do what he did. Talk yourself into an entry-level job. Watch closely. Give careful thought to where you can contribute. Speak respectfully and politely to your superiors — being a smart-ass may be cool in school but it doesn't work well in real life — and show you are really interested in the job. Ask questions by the hundreds. Do research in the evenings. Ask more questions. Show them you are interested in business, and in their business in particular.

Remember, by the way, that not asking questions and not showing any interest tells your employer a great deal about you. Regardless of the business, taking a sincere interest goes a long way. You will be amazed what you can learn about companies, agencies, human relations, business operations, and management styles simply by being alert and attentive.

If you approach your first job as a learning experience, as well as a way to make some money, you will benefit enormously. You'll find out much more about what you like and dislike — sales or human resources, warehouse operations or being a waiter — and you'll discover where you have special skills and aptitudes. This is a trial-and-error approach that carries very little risk and considerable potential benefit. Imagine going to college or university and then discovering that you dislike your chosen field (this happens a lot to teachers and lawyers, if they can find work at all these days). Give work a chance and grow along with it.

DON'T FORGET WHAT IT'S ABOUT: MAKING MONEY

Work is, in the end, about making money. You will hear a lot of self-actualization stuff about finding a job you truly love or doing something that develops your full potential. Lovely, if you can get it. Most people go to work to pay the bills. They may not get much satisfaction in collecting garbage, filing legal papers, shelving groceries, or handling government forms, but they need to make a living and they try to find the best job that they can. Our guess is that around 10 percent of all working people have jobs that they really enjoy or that brings out the best in them. Most others just earn a living. You need to as well. So if you decide to take this approach after high school and go looking for a job, tackle the experience as an exercise in money management.

The brutal truth about minimum wage is that it's a life of poverty, or semi-poverty. The minimum wage in Canada is around $10 an hour, with some variation from province to province (some permit a lower one for beginners). Forty hours of work per week brings in $400, fifty-two weeks a year with a couple of weeks off amounts to $20,000 before federal and provincial income taxes. Suppose you end up with $16,000. Can you live on that, outside your parents' basement? Our bottom line here is that it's fine to take a minimum-wage part-time job while you're in high school because it's a good way to learn about the world of work, and if you can't think of anything to do after high school, it's probably better to take this kind of job than lie around the house playing computer games. But it's a lousy plan for the long term.

FIND A JOB WITH IMPACT

Getting a job right out of high school need not mean taking any minimum-wage opportunity that comes along, but you have to be realistic. Few places outside a few high-wage, high-cost communities in the western Canadian oil patch are going to pay $20 an hour for unskilled workers. There are great opportunities in the retail and service industries — admittedly the kinds of jobs most parents and guidance counsellors sneer at a little — and jobs that could really expand your horizons and give you deeper insights into the world around you. Do things you haven't done before. This is an experiment, after all, and it's designed to help you learn about yourself.

Consider some of these possibilities:

- **Work with animals** — at a veterinary clinic, a zoo, a ranch, or the local animal pound.

- **Work with seniors** — the number of homes and activity centres for seniors is growing by the week. Senior have amazing stories to tell and being with them can deliver a much-needed jolt of humility.

- **Work with new Canadians** — there are hundreds of not-for-profit centres offering settlement services for recent immigrants to Canada. These folks really need friendly, kind, and knowledgeable people to help them. A fair bit of the work involves looking after children, through language lessons and babysitting.

- **Work with children** — while most of the jobs in the field are now filled by people with college diplomas and university degrees, there are private daycares, private schools, and the like that offer the chance to work with children.

- **Find a basic job in a professional office** — every law firm, architecture office (our favourite), and accounting company has basic jobs that have to be done, from filing and delivering mail to completing forms. These are remarkable places to be around. The people are smart and engaging, and often like to mentor young folks. (In major American firms, by the way, these jobs are going to university graduates.)

- **Get an entry-level job with a not-for-profit organization** — each community has many charities and other not-for-profit agencies. These low-budget operations often need help with basic tasks. They can provide you with an excellent window into a complex world that most people never see.

- **Work in construction** — while the well-paid jobs require a formal trade or certificate, most construction sites need someone to clean up, load and unload supplies, and otherwise support construction activity. You may find that there is benefit in physical labour and real pleasure being part of the construction of something new. Start your search with small contractors or renovators.

- **Find a job with a moving company** — if you have a strong back and like large-scale puzzles, a job with a moving firm can be attractive. The work is demanding, but the challenge of getting goods in and out of trucks and homes can be quite intriguing.

You get the point. There are jobs available for unskilled, entry-level workers. You have to work hard to find a job — college and university graduates are shouldering their way into the positions that used to be left over for people coming out of high school — but there are possibilities out there. Find something that stretches you or that tests something you are considering for a career. Walking down the street to the fast food store shows a desire to earn and to work, but does not show much initiative or creativity.

By the way, many employees with these organizations start as volunteers. So, if you are thinking about any of these opportunities for a full-time job after high school, consider volunteering with them in grade eleven or grade twelve.

PROVE YOURSELF THROUGH WORK

Contrary to what you have been told repeatedly by parents, teachers, and others, you have a lot to learn and are largely unproven. Graduating from high school, even with an 80 percent average, is no great shakes. That makes you only a little impressive. You are not likely going to set the world on fire, find the job of your dreams, or soar with the eagles. Life just isn't like that, and all of the self-esteem building exercises you have been through have done you a grave disservice.

Here are the top five things that most young people of this generation have to prove. You don't necessarily have to prove all of them, but you do have to prove some:

- **that you can tackle real and sustained challenges** — academic, technical, or otherwise;

- **that you can succeed on your own**, without parental intervention or special conditions;

- **that you are capable of hard work** on a regular basis;

- **that you have realistic expectations** about your abilities and responsibilities;

- **that you can handle hard physical labour.**

Half a century ago, only a small percentage of people finished high school and only a few went to university. Now, young people are almost forced to graduate from high school and are pushed strongly toward college, polytechnic, or university. Regardless of which route you take, consider this your declaration of independence. To this point, most of you have relied very heavily on parents, teachers, and other adult mentors to make your decisions and to shape your lives. Now the safety net is gone and you are on your own. Many of you will delay this process, either by staying at home or by going to college or university, as selected and paid for by your parents. Indeed, young North Americans have gotten into the habit of prolonging their dependence on their parents into their late twenties and sometimes beyond.

Resist this, if for no other reason than that employers and others evaluating your file like to see signs of early independence. Once again, think about an employer choosing between two comparable candidates. One struck out on her own after high school, found work, moved out of the family house, and then presented herself for a job opportunity. The other stayed at home, still relies heavily on parental financial support, eats for free, and uses the family laundry and other facilities. Which of these people would you think an employer would see as more responsible, self-reliant, and mature? We know which one we would select.

As you see, we have strong views on this topic. Young Canadians, in our experience, have a deeply flawed work ethic. Jobs are hard, even the ones that are not physically or emotionally demanding. It's not easy to take orders from others, especially if you think they're idiots, as they may well be. Showing up at work — on time, in a good mood, ready to work even if you aren't — isn't easy either. But life is no walk in the park and it's vital that you understand this as soon as you possibly can.

WHAT WE DID

We took different approaches to work when we were young. Bill spent high school summers in the army reserves, starting at age fifteen (he lied about his age to get in, though of course we don't endorse lying), then worked driving an ice-cream truck the summer after his first year of university, saving enough to spend the next summer in Europe. He then got his ideal summer job, as a member of the Fort Henry Guard at Kingston. This work involved drilling, firing the large guns, and giving tours, and culminated in a trip to the Royal Tournament in London and then to Expo 67.

Ken always worked — delivering papers, mowing lawns, shovelling driveways, and learning that the extra things he wanted from life — mostly outdoor gear and baseball gloves — were better if earned through hard work. His first real job, as a librarian's assistant, combined the formalities of a job with his deep love of reading. But then, between years of university, he worked on highway crews and in fishing camps.

Both of us worked while we went to university — Ken at gym kiosks and Bill as a residence don in graduate school. And we like to think that we developed and/ or possessed a strong work ethic that has served us well into adulthood.

DON'T UNDERESTIMATE WHERE WORK CAN TAKE YOU

Some of you have had very privileged lives, others much less so. Canada is one of those countries where all of you have an opportunity to progress to the highest levels in the workforce, the professions, and public life. But the honest truth is that this country does not exhibit perfect equality. Those who are born rich will likely die rich. Teenagers from middle- and upper-middle-class backgrounds have huge advantages over those from the working poor or welfare families. For most of you, the path forward has been sketched out, if not fully defined, by the time you leave high school.

But work can be the great equalizer. A well-to-do, highly educated person who does not work well with others is likely to crash and burn (unless his parents own the business, in which case life really is not fair). A young adult from a disadvantaged background who possesses a strong work ethic and has the ability to apply her skills will generally do well in life. The reality is that work is where expectations, abilities, and effort collide — producing winners and losers in the great economic race that is modern Canadian life.

Here are two closing bits of advice. First, if you already have a university degree, and are holding down a McJob, get out of it as soon as you can. There's nothing wrong with your job, but unless want to make a career of it, leave it asap. This book gives all sorts of advice that is applicable to your situation, and you should look especially hard at the college and polytech options, though a bit of volunteering wouldn't hurt either. But don't stay where you are, unless your heart is set on the food or retail service sector. That's fine, but if you wanted service as a career, you wouldn't have gone to university in the first place, would you?

And finally, don't take your mother to a job interview. Believe it or not, many young people do this — and parents have been known to follow up after the interview, often to complain about their child not being hired. Make your job hunt your own, and handle the interview processes yourself. Consider this Test One of whether you're really ready to step away from the nest. If you're not, then we're officially worried about you!

CHAPTER TEN

APPRENTICESHIPS
AND THE SKILLED TRADES

FIND OUT ABOUT APPRENTICESHIPS

In some countries — Germany is a good example — apprenticeships in the trades and technical fields are central to the education system, the economy, and middle-class prosperity. In Canada, unfortunately, apprenticeships are a seriously neglected option for young adults. In the last two years the federal government, increasingly preoccupied with correcting the "skills imbalance" in Canada, has begun to offset the general disfavour in which apprenticeships and the skilled trades are held. Basically, the government wants more young Canadians — that's you — trained for the skilled trades so that we can lessen our dependence on imported labour. Let's hope this effort succeeds, for the skilled trades offer strong career possibilities, good incomes, and interesting and demanding work.

An apprenticeship is essentially a matchmaking arrangement that brings together someone who wants to develop a specific skill with an employer who is looking for a worker and is willing to provide training. Most of the work — 90 percent in most cases — takes place on the job, with the rest being done before, during, or after at a training institution. There are more than three hundred different apprenticeship programs in Canada, covering a wide variety of trades: welder, Aboriginal childhood development practitioner, baker, alarm and security technician, composite material laminator, florist, hair stylist, and many more. Each apprenticeship has entrance requirements (hint: keep up the high school math), but the focus is on the development of specialized skills through direct participation and careful oversight by an experienced tradesperson.

The apprenticeship system works in the opposite direction from the standard college-polytechnic-university system. At a college, polytechnic, or university, students explore areas of interest, graduate, and then try to match themselves with an employer. With an apprenticeship, the initial matchmaking occurs at the beginning, before the work and training begin. It's not uncommon for high school students who are proficient in the skilled trades to start working on their apprenticeship while in school and proceed directly into a paid position after graduating.

These apprenticeships, which can take as little as one and as much as five years, typically involve paid employment (at a lower rate than for a fully credentialed skilled tradesperson). In some trades, you can start the apprenticeship in high school or, particularly in Quebec, do most of your classroom training before you start the work experience. At the end, apprentices receive their full qualification in the form of a journeyperson certificate or similar designation. The certificate is the marketable piece — the apprentice is not tied to the employer for life and can now move freely within the industry and across the country on the basis of possessing a well-understood set of skills and abilities.

THE JOYS OF WORKING WITH YOUR HANDS

In the distant past, we used to celebrate the talents and work ethic of the small farmer, who was seen as the backbone of Western civilization. Most of them are now gone, replaced by industrial-sized mega-farms. We then passed through a time when the skilled tradesperson — factory worker, construction worker, equipment operator — was seen as core to Canadian prosperity. These jobs are still around, but our attentions have shifted to more sedentary, cleaner, and more clerical work.

There are all kinds of jobs that are decent and have merit — whether it's filling out forms or repairing airplanes, writing computer code or building a new church, working in a bank or operating a gas plant. There is, however, something special about working with your hands, creating new things, repairing stuff, and keeping machinery humming. Tradespeople make vital contributions to our collective well-being — and they often enjoy and take great pride in their work. Look at construction workers at the final stages of a housing or office construction project, or oil rig operators when they strike oil, or electrical workers as they scramble to re-establish power lines after a storm. There is tremendous value in having the ability to work with tools and technology, to solve practical, real-world problems, and to build and maintain things.

For a great way to find opportunities, spend some time exploring options through the Ellis Chart, a comparative chart of apprentice training programs across Canada produced by Human Resources and Skills Development Canada in partnership with the Canadian Council of Directors of Apprenticeship (CCDA).[1] Because this is Canada, there are thirteen different apprenticeship systems available, with somewhat compatible but not identical requirements and regulations. The country does have the Red Seal Program, designed to ensure "an interprovincial standard of excellence for the skilled trades prized by employers." It uses examinations to establish common standards to facilitate interprovincial recognition of credentials, and is overseen by the CCDA.

Apprenticeship programs don't have automatic entry. Remember that employers are making a real — and expensive — commitment to the apprentice in terms of wages, oversight, and training. They hope and expect that the apprentice will stay on with them after getting the certification, which means that there is a high correlation between being taken on as an apprentice and having an ongoing job at a decent income.

Here's how the system works in the construction industry. You can find a sponsor for your apprenticeship by finding an employer yourself, going through a union, or approaching the apprenticeship and training committee in your province and in the sector of your choice. Most employers want you to have at least a high school diploma, not because it necessarily prepares you for anything but as proof that you can stick to and finish a task. Your work experience is monitored very closely and documented by the employer, particularly in those fields called "compulsory trades" where everyone working in a trade has to be in a certified apprenticeship program. You are responsible for the classroom part of your program, which is generally not paid for by the employer. Apprentices are paid between 30 and 50 percent of the regular wage of the certified journeyperson at the beginning, with increases possible as skill level rises. Most construction apprentices work about 80 percent of the year and take courses during the rest.

DON'T SHY AWAY FROM PHYSICAL WORK

Apprenticeships are attractive for a number of reasons:

- **They lead to good jobs,** with a decent starting wage (remember you are unskilled when you start).

- **They provide on-the-job training** with expert supervision and a lot of practice.

- **They include classroom instruction** to provide the technical background that you require. Don't underestimate the challenges of the classroom work. This is real-world stuff, with much less margin for error than in a first-year biology or sociology class. These courses are often very demanding, and rightly so.

You may be wondering why you weren't told about this. The answer is simple: far too many Canadians shy away from working with their hands. This country was built on the backs of men and women who worked as cooks, welders, pipefitters, carpenters, electricians, and mechanics. Despite the current craze for "white-collar" careers, these jobs and many like them are as important now as they ever were, and they are often well paid.

To learn a trade was once a standard Canadian option, particularly for people from working-class backgrounds and for new Canadians. With the resource and industrial sectors booming in the decades after the Second World War, working with one's hands was a well-paid and attractive way of life (it still is for those not blinded by the lure of a university degree). For people newly arrived in this country, moving from rural areas to the cities, or coming of age in the booming Canadian economy, the opportunity to work in a skilled trade and find employment (often in a unionized shop) in the auto sector, forestry, general manufacturing, construction, health care, and many other fields was highly attractive. These jobs paid well and required hard and highly technical work. Skilled tradespeople were valued by employers and took great pride in their work, as they still do.

But the skilled trades seem to have lost their buzz in Canada. While swarms of young Canadians head to university, college, and polytechnic programs for which they are often ill suited, the country's companies scour the world for skilled tradespeople. In the resource sector, in particular, Canada is once again doing what it did in the 1950s and 1960s: importing thousands of highly skilled immigrants to take jobs that too few Canadians are trained to fill.

Of course, all Canadians want the "good life," however they define it. But in these uncertain times, they tend to swarm like Toronto commuters on the infamous highway 401, all heading in the same direction but increasingly jammed together. Right now, that direction is focused on office work. But if you think that's the ideal life, start reading Dilbert cartoons or watch *The Office* on TV. Forget Google and Apple. They're the fantasy employers, with their campus-like atmosphere, games rooms, and free cafeterias — but you won't likely get to play games with them. In Canada, not surprisingly, working for the federal government is pretty high on the list. It's what the Chinese call the "iron rice bowl" — safe, secure, well-paid jobs with excellent benefits — but there are lots of pointy-headed bosses there too. Not enough young people grow up aspiring to be machinists or pipefitters, despite the demand for these trades and the good wages associated with them.

And not many parents push their children in these directions, even if such important work has deep roots within their families. For the majority of Canadian parents, "rescuing" their children from a life of physical labour appears to be a high ambition. It's not that they dislike the skilled trades. Goodness knows they call on plumbers, electricians, and carpenters to fix things, and most know that the skilled tradespeople are crucial to the economy. It has more to do with core values and expectations.

Parents usually want better lives for their children than they had themselves — and not having to work with your hands is part of this dream. It's an odd way to look at the world. A plumber typically makes more money and has more interesting, problem-solving work than a clerk in a government office. But in our day and age, white-collar work — with a cubicle and desk or, if you are really good, an office of your own — is perceived as high-quality and valuable, while working with your hands is less attractive and less valued, even though it may pay more.

Remember, too, that your parents have been living for the past thirty years in a world dominated by talk of the end of physical work (machines will do it all), the importance of the "knowledge economy," and the surging fortunes (with a few bumps) of the digital media, finance, and government sectors. There is something in what they say. The right person with the right skills and good luck can grab a fabulous job with a bank, a trading firm, or a high technology company — but that same person, with lesser skills or not such good luck, can end up taking airline reservations over the telephone until she is replaced by online systems.

Understand where your parents are coming from — but if the skilled trades attract you, hold your ground. There are great opportunities as an apprentice and the investment of time can be truly rewarding.

The real reasons young Canadians are not directed in large numbers to the trades are simple:

- **We tend to avoid physical labour** where we can.

- **We're so urban in character** that many young people grow up without much hands-on experience with fixing cars and tractors, operating outboard motors, working on construction, and other tasks that develop facility with and interest in skilled trades.

- **We've been influenced by years of complaints and criticism from environmental groups directed at the natural resource sector.** As a result, work in that sector, once celebrated as the centre of the Canadian economy, has been undermined. Canadians haven't stopped consuming huge quantities of natural resources, but we don't want to actually work to extract them.

CONSIDER THE FINANCIAL BENEFITS OF APPRENTICESHIP

As with any part of the economy, there are no guarantees with apprenticeship programs. Companies run into financial difficulties, sectors expand and contract, jobs come and go. Right now, there are terrific opportunities in the skilled trades, particularly in western Canada and specifically in the natural resource sector. Apprenticeships are usually offered in areas where there are solid and continuing employment possibilities, thereby giving you a clear indication of future prospects. Many former apprentices go on to establish their own businesses, either as independent operators or as owners of companies. Starting as an apprentice is often an excellent way to build up practical experience and, by watching closely, develop an understanding of how the industry operates. Many successful Canadian business people started their careers as apprentices in the skilled trades.

An apprenticeship can lead to lucrative, full-time work or to lower-paid but still valuable employment. Not many bicycle mechanics and chefs make $150,000 a year, but neither do schoolteachers. A substantial number of gasfitters, crane operators, and pipefitters can pull in big bucks, particularly on northern and western resource projects. Most people who make the transition from apprentice to journeyperson earn decent incomes, although they, too, are vulnerable to downturns in the local economy or the closure of a manufacturing plant.

Remember that income starts at the very beginning of the apprenticeship. While your college- and university-bound friends are spending their own or their parents' money on tuition and books, you're earning a wage from your first day of work (with breaks in earning when you take your turn in school). Apprentices often complete their program with little or no debt, which puts them quite a few steps ahead of those who took alternate routes. People in the skilled trades have the added advantage of being mobile, both in Canada and internationally.

HERE'S A QUICK TEST

Go to Google and type in "Qatar" and "pipefitter." Look at the list of employers in this small Middle Eastern country looking for tradespeople. The advantage of having a tightly controlled system is that although it can be tough to get the apprenticeship in the first instance, the credential, once earned, travels extremely well and can open doors literally around the world.

PICK THE RIGHT APPRENTICESHIP PROGRAM

Like everything else we've discussed, apprenticeships and the skilled trades are not for everyone. Some people are simply not made out to be heavy equipment repair specialists, drafts-people, arborists, or four-colour sheet-fed offset press operators. It is vital that you know yourself and be familiar with the field that you are considering. Spend time investigating the various skilled trades. Companies looking for employees often attend career and job fairs. Give them a serious amount of time. Don't expect to be actively recruited. Unlike the universities that will fall over you with fancy brochures and attractive recruitment stories, the skilled trades are looking for very practical people who are not drawn by glitter.

If you see something you like, ask to visit the workplace. Spend a day or two shadowing a journey-person in the field — they're often very keen to see a young person interested in their specialty. If you can, build an apprenticeship option into your high school program; it will provide you with a head start if you decide to go down this path and will provide you with valuable work experience if you opt for a different career. If you're keen enough, an employer might hire you for a part-time or summer job, giving you a chance to explore the sector in even greater detail.

The key here — as always — is finding the right match. Employers want young people who know how to work, have the aptitude for a skilled trade, and are interested in self-improvement. You want a position that will lead to a decent career, with a solid income and some long-term flexibility. We wish more Canadian young people would consider apprenticeships. The government of Canada is making a real effort to promote youth participation in the skilled trades through grants and other means. The companies are eager if you are.

So here's the bottom line. Skilled tradespeople really know how to work. They're proud of their abilities, have sophisticated skills, keep up with developments in their industry, and don't like being looked down upon by the white-collar brigade, especially when they have higher incomes than office workers do. They generally like their work and are good at it. Approach the skilled trades with the respect that they deserve. It can be hard work, but it's very good work, with significant prospects for personal growth and prosperity. Reject the idea that there's something wrong with working with your hands in the trades. That is rubbish. For the right people, apprenticeships and the skilled trades are dynamite options.

CHAPTER ELEVEN

PREPARING FOR LIFE AFTER HIGH SCHOOL

NOW WHAT DO YOU DO?

If you've stayed with us this far, good for you! Hopefully, you now have a better sense of who you are and what you should do next. In these last three chapters, we will give you the tools to make the best of the time you have left before graduation. We will offer you some guidelines for how to optimize the time you spend preparing yourself for whatever comes next and, finally, we will present a framework in which you can situate yourself and your future.

Despite our efforts to the contrary, we know that some of you will follow the swarm to university and will join those who actually should be there. For that reason — and, frankly, because that's where our experience is strongest — we are going to focus here on the ways in you can best prepare yourself for university. It is important to remember, though, that the suggestions we are making here also are relevant — in some way — to any of the paths open to you. Becoming good at math, for example, may not seem to be particularly important to you if you're setting out to travel or committing yourself to a year of volunteerism. But the disciplined, rigorous thinking needed for advanced math can help you to organize your efforts so that you achieve your desired outcome.

ARE YOU READY FOR SUCCESS?

Let's assume that you have passed the curiosity test and made the decision to go to university — a decision made alone, with your parents, or as a result of broader pressure to attend. The next question that arises logically is this: are you ready? We are sorry to have to tell you that, for large numbers of young people, the answer is *no*. Coming to university when you are not fully prepared is a really bad idea that can lead to a great deal of unhappiness. However, coming when you are keen and ready can be a real joy. Preparation helps, as does self-awareness.

Here are the top five conditions for success at university:

- **High school grades are important**, though they are not guarantees of success. The research shows that high-achieving high school students do well in university. Students who come to university with an average in the mid to high eighties will, in general, do well — though their grades will likely fall substantially (two-thirds of first-year students get lower grades than they did in their last year of high school).[1] While individual circumstances vary, students who come to university with a high school average of 75 percent or lower have a fairly small chance of succeeding in their studies, and many of those with less than 80 percent will also struggle. Time and effort spent in high school do pay off.

- **English or French language writing ability is one of the most important predictors of career success.** There are no short-cuts here. You must be able to read and write effectively. This is one of the greatest shortcomings of today's university students. Too many students devote great effort to their mathematical and scientific skills and much less to writing. This is a huge mistake. Learn to write well. If your mother tongue is other than English or French, we are impressed with your ability to learn another language or two. But students with English as a Second Language often have serious problems at the university level, where tolerance for bad grammar, poor spelling, and awkward sentence construction is typically very low. Don't rush to university if you barely passed the English or French language entrance standard.

- **Mathematics matters.** All high school students wanting to get into top university programs should have completed academic mathematics courses through to grade twelve, including calculus if available. There are two major reasons for doing so. First, numeracy matters and is of fundamental importance to many of the fastest-growing, best-paying careers around — from such obvious scientifically based fields as nanotechnology to areas such as finance, accounting, and economics. Second, mathematics is a very good indication of overall intellectual ability. Math is challenging, tricky, innovative, and creative. Other courses in high school have similar qualities, but you do not require high-end skills to get top grades in many of them. If you can do well in math (and not simply by taking the same course two or three times, as in the notorious high school "victory lap"), you have demonstrated the capacity for hard, intellectually demanding work.

- **Reading (a lot) is key.** This was part of the "curiosity test" and is, we think, vitally important. An amazing number of young adults do not read newspapers, magazines, non-fiction books, high-quality literature, or serious blogs or Internet-based commentary. Fewer than one-quarter of all university students in the United States read as much as a single book per year above specific course requirements. We find this sad and depressing. Canadian students are much the same. Literate young people are engaged and often well informed. The best university students read a lot. If you do not read on a regular basis, the chances that you will find university interesting are quite small. Note, by the way, that reading is strongly correlated with writing ability. Good readers are typically strong writers. Read. Read some more. Then keep reading. We have a longer section on this later.

UNIVERSITY READINESS CHECKLIST

- I am naturally curious
- I have strong grades (above 80 percent, and 90 percent for elite university programs)
- I write well and I enjoy writing
- I am good at math
- I am a reader
- I am self-motivated

If you are six for six, you will likely have your choice of universities and your pick of many top programs. But if you miss on one or more of these items, take a long, hard look at yourself. Are you really ready for success at university?

- **Self-motivation is essential.** Students who rely on parents and teachers to get their work done are at risk in university. After high school, students are pretty much on their own — and some find this difficult to deal with. Professors do not often check to see if you attend classes or nag you to get your assignments done on time. If you count on your parents to get you up for school and meet your deadlines, and if you depend on teachers to make sure you stay on course in your studies, you don't have the work habits you need for university studies. This is not — by the way — a skill set that you can really wait until after high school to develop in full. Top athletes push their coaches as much as the other way around. Accomplished musicians do not need to be reminded to practise. The best students approach their studies with the same energy and commitment.

HAVE YOU PLANNED PROPERLY?

You are about to make one of the most important decisions of your life. How much time have you devoted to this decision? Canadians are pretty easy-going about their choice of university — probably because, in contrast to the American situation, the universities are easy to get into if you have halfway decent high school grades. Indeed, most young people just sort of fall into both the choice to attend university and the selection of the institution (typically it is the one closest to home). Families in other countries make this into a decade-long saving and planning enterprise.

Check out what happens in other countries. Wealthy American families spend tens of thousands of dollars on college coaches, test-writing seminars, campus visits, and the like. The struggle to get into the elite institutions is a national obsession. In China, in the battle to get into the best universities (Nanjing University accepts only one of every thousand applicants), children study relentlessly for their last two years of high school in order to make top grades. Hundreds of thousands of families around the world save for years so that one or more of their children can attend a well-regarded foreign institution — like the ones that you have available to you for surprisingly little effort.

What is the Canadian equivalent to all of this angst and worry? You fill in an online form, type in your parents' credit card number, and wait for the letter(s) of offer, with a fairly high level of confidence that all will work out well. But will it all work out? Will you make the right decision to go, or not to? And if you go, will you go to the right place and choose the right program? It's easy enough to get in to a Canadian university, true enough, but getting in is only a first minor step that does not guarantee you the life you may be looking for.

Here are eight major steps that you should take to prepare properly to make the right choices:

- **Keep your options open in high school.** Teenagers often make rash decisions in high school: dropping academic math for an extra computer class, avoiding language courses, and worrying as much about protecting spares as the content of the courses they take. Do not take the easy road. Remember that university, if you go, will be much harder and more demanding than high school. Take a full course load, take demanding and high-quality courses, and make sure that you do not close off your academic options. For example, if you do not complete the right grade twelve math courses, you could find yourself denied access to many of the most attractive programs on many university and college campuses.

- **Establish a history of work.** Quite surprisingly, at least 25 percent of all of the students who enroll in the University of Waterloo's co-operative education program arrive at university without work experience. Nowadays there is no substitute for experience. It is vital that you work during the latter stages of high school and that you find jobs that have some relationship to the kind of future that you envisage. If you are interested in becoming an entrepreneur, look into starting a summer business. If you are keen about working in construction, get a job as a handyperson's helper. Whatever you choose to do — get a job, do it well, demonstrate that you are a hard and effective worker, and earn a positive recommendation.

- **Volunteer.** While some cynical students look at volunteer work as a way of building a résumé — helpful if you expect to be competitive for law or medical school — there are many great reasons for all young adults to volunteer. First, establishing a pattern of giving and helping is good for the soul — it both builds and reflects your character. Second, volunteer activities provide leadership opportunities and can give you excellent practice in a variety of semi-professional areas. Opt for something that involves organizational responsibilities or technical work, like being a treasurer for a school club. These kinds of commitments reveal a great deal about your personality and your general abilities.

- **Explore the world of work.** It is always astonishing to talk to young adults who have decided to prepare for a career that they know only in the abstract. Learn as much as you can about the fields of endeavour you are considering. Attend career days. Go to job fairs. Check the websites for Human Resources Development Canada, or the trade unions, or *workopolis.com* and *monster.ca*. Job shadow as often as you can (your parents' friends, community members, and neighbours often provide great opportunities). If you are interested in the law, sit in the public section of a courtroom and watch the law in action (be prepared to be bored; it's not like TV). The best teachers are often those who volunteer in elementary school classes while still in high school. They at least know what they are getting into. Many professional associations or trade unions are keen to help young people learn about opportunities in their fields. Remember, as you go about this process, that eliminating options — you thought you might be a teacher, but then you decide that dealing with thirty adolescents in a class is an unattractive proposition — is as important as identifying precisely what you do want to do.

- **Be wise about money.** Universities and colleges in Canada, contrary to public belief, are not a huge drain on your resources — unless you are from a low-income family, at which point they can be prohibitively expensive. Unfortunately, students and families are often ill-informed about what the actual costs are. Tuition costs are only part of the total expense, particularly if the student is living away from home. Attending university means making significant sacrifices in standard of living. You are at university to study and improve yourself, and you cannot and should not live as though you are fully employed (i.e., no fancy car unless your parents are wealthy and indulgent). Smart young people heading to university have given careful thought to the sources of funding (parents, employment, government loans and grants, scholarships and bursaries) and the real expenses associated with going to school. Spend a lot of time planning your budget and considering the alternatives. And if you decide not to go to university, the time and effort spent on budgeting will stand you in good stead as you make the transition to the workforce.

- **Pay attention to the world around you.** Watch what is happening in our country's trading relations with China. Keep tabs on the progress of the American economy. See what is happening with the resource sector in western Canada. Keep a critical eye on what people say about the future. These are not just news items of interest to your parents. They will define your future prospects and opportunities. There are patterns amidst all of the noise and debates, and you have to find the part of the broader picture that works for you.

- **Explore alternatives.** Plan to devote a substantial amount of time over your last two years of high school to considering all of the options, many of which are described in this book. Consider colleges, universities, apprenticeships, the world of work, and the other alternatives that we describe. This is your life. Take charge of it.

- **Do a full accounting of the entire cost of the choices that you are considering.** First, be understanding of your parents. If they are footing the bill for your advanced education (for many Canadian students, grandparents are putting in money as well), they are making major sacrifices. Be respectful of their sacrifices and commitment to you. It might help explain why they believe that have a major stake in your decision. Second, make sure you include lost income in your financial planning. If you headed into the work-force right after high school, you would likely get only an entry-level job, perhaps in a coffee shop or grocery store. At the Canadian minimum wage (assume it is $10 an hour), you would earn about $20,000 a year. If you take five years to complete a degree, you will have lost $100,000 in income. So, the degree, at $15,000 a year in direct expenses, is actually going to cost you (or someone) a total of $175,000, minus whatever you earn in part-time and summer work. If you spend this money on your education and end up selling coffee or stocking shelves anyway, you will have made a major investment in your education for a very small financial return.

To us, this advice seems pretty obvious, and we know from our experience with the thousands of young adults we have known over the years that it works. It is easy to differentiate between young people with real potential and the ones marking time as they work their way through their courses and programs. Here is the key point: in the not-so-distant past, the simple fact that someone had a university degree answered an employer's most important questions about an application. In 1960, having a degree generally meant that you were intelligent, motivated, endowed with good work habits, reliable and dependable, innately curious, and well organized.

But now the university entrance gates have swung almost completely open — just see how many of your high school friends (some of whom, you will agree, were hardly stellar in class) are going to university. As the universities have accepted a much broader range of students, the ability of an employer to assume that a degree represented all of these personal qualities has diminished. A university degree still means something: it does require persistence, a certain level of skill and — depending on the field — good deal of ability. But it might not mean this, and that is why you need much more in your résumé if you expect to get noticed.

If you've decided at this point that university is for you, we want to prepare you the best way we know how to make it a huge success. Remember, if you want the career you are hoping for, you must be able to stand apart from the swarm. The time to prepare for this success is now — well, actually, the time to start was several years ago, but now is still better than never.

HOW CAN YOU GET (OR SHARPEN) THESE ESSENTIAL SKILLS?

It would be nice if everything we said could be upbeat, and if we could tell you nothing but sweet things: you are the greatest generation that ever lived, your education so far has been first-rate, you are fully equipped for university, where you will succeed and make your parents proud. University won't be too difficult, because you were an A student in high school, with an 80 percent average, and so on and so on. But we won't lie to you: all of this may be true, or some of it, or none of it. Only you can judge (until, of course, your university judges you).

There are, though, two things that are essential to your success in university. They also will significantly improve your chances for success in whatever you do in your life.

LEARN TO WRITE

Let's start with the conclusion to this part: there is nothing — not anything — more fundamental to success in an English-speaking university than the ability to write English prose. This is true in the sciences as well in the humanities. It's probably less true if you are aiming for a degree in physical education (more important there to have athletic ability, but you will still be surprised), but it's vital everywhere else. Allied with this is the ability to read fluently and critically. Yes, of course you can read and write. We aren't suggesting that you are illiterate. But can you read and write at a university level? A dismaying number of university students can't — a fact that illuminates one of the great failures of our contemporary primary and secondary education system.

On the subject of writing, we have good news and bad news. The good news is that, given practice, anyone can learn to write in a manner that will be acceptable to those who grade undergraduate essays and research papers in the various disciplines. There are a number of different styles used at university: papers written for the humanities and social sciences are not the same as those written for the physical sciences, where "scientific writing" is required. But it can all be learned, if you want to learn it. Be warned, however, that universities do not want the compositions that you wrote in high school. They do not care how you spent your summer vacation, nor are they interested in what a colourful character your grandfather was. They want evidence of research and analysis, clearly and correctly put forward in prose.

We assume here that you really want to learn to write, that you are going to take writing seriously, and not just scrape through with C- grades along with the swarm, or — heaven forbid — buy your essays from some criminal Internet source. (Shame on those who do this — universities and other institutions have clever ways in which to catch them, and they deserve the heavy penalties that await them if caught.)

Before we tell you how to learn to write, we should explain why correct writing is necessary. You may have experienced some fussy teacher, a stuffy pedant who tells you silly stuff such as the "rule" that you should never end a sentence with a preposition. Someone once said that to Winston Churchill, who replied "this is the kind of nonsense up with which I will not put." (If you don't know what a preposition is, then you have a point at which to start learning.) That's not what we mean, and it's not even, contrary to what English teachers will tell you, that you have to write well to make your meaning clear. Of course you do, but you'd have to be pretty awful to write in a way such that a reader couldn't tell what you were talking about, though we have read some student papers of this kind.

The harsh fact is that the way you write is a marker of your education and, to some extent, of your class background — much as Canadians like to pretend that social class does not exist in this country. Example: if you write *I don't know nothing about it*, English teachers will recoil in horror (we will too), though your meaning is perfectly clear (pedants will say that *I don't know nothing* means that you do know something, but that's just pedantry). The reason that it's wrong to say this is a social one: it makes you sound uneducated. Do you want to sound like a doofus when you submit a university paper, apply for a job, or write a letter or an email during the course of your employment? Do you want people to roll their eyes when they read your writing? Surely not, and that's why you want to write correctly. The rules of correct English writing are not carved in stone, and they do change over time: they are simply the usages that educated people and good writers have decided upon, and though the preposition thing is not one of them, the rule against double negatives is.

How, then, do you learn to write? It's simple, but not necessarily easy, and here is the bad news we mentioned above. The best way to learn to write is not to study the rules of English grammar — the difference between and principal and a subordinate clause, and all the others. You will want to do this, but later on. Here's the secret: to learn to write, you have to internalize the structure and rhythms of the written English language, and the best and probably the only way to do this is to read. Read, and read, and read, and read. Read good fiction, good non-fiction, read as much as you can, read a book or two a week, not drivel like zombie novels written for adolescents, but fiction by masters of English from past years such as Jane Austen, Ernest Hemingway and John Steinbeck, or, to pick modern Canadian examples, Tom King, Mordecai Richler, Margaret Atwood, or Alice Munro (a wonderful writer of short stories who just won the Nobel Prize for literature). Have you ever read *The Apprenticeship of Duddy Kravitz, The Grapes of Wrath*, or *The Handmaid's Tale?* Were they assigned high school reading? If so, you probably viewed them as a chore. But read them again, carefully, and see how the sentences and paragraphs are constructed. Listen to the rhythm of the words. You are not going to write like these people, and neither are we — nor would we want to. But they are masters of English prose, and you can learn from them. Don't try to learn from the writers of earlier generations. You want to write in a modern fashion, not like Charles Dickens. Read twentieth- and twenty-first-century stuff.

Read good non-fiction. There's so much of it that it's hard to know what to recommend, but after a while you will recognize it. As the U.S. Supreme Court justice said about pornography, you will find it hard to define, but you will know it when you see it. Ask someone you respect to recommend some reading in a field that interests you. Read a book a week, two books a week, and eventually you will internalize what good English sounds like. Once you know that, you will be able to write. After that you can learn the rules of grammar. It's appalling that many high schools no longer teach them, but that's another story.

And then you should write. You will of course write all your high school assignments, but some schools don't give very many, and some go in for the composition type of thing that doesn't do you any good at university. Why not write for the school yearbook or, even better, become the school correspondent for your local newspaper? Write wherever you can: news in the bulletin of your temple, church, or mosque, something about your hockey team for the newspaper. Write letters to your elderly relatives who don't use the computer. Have someone whose literacy skills you trust look over your writing and comment on it. Yes, all this is work, but you want to stand out from the swarm, don't you?

How long will it take to learn to write? Well, a good time to start is as early as possible, as soon as you actually learn to read. Six years old is about right. Most great writers were voracious readers from their youth. But it's never too late, and if you start now and read and write consistently, you can become a decent writer, turning out essays and research papers that, if not Hemingway-esque, will at least not embarrass you.

We say again: there is nothing, not anything, more fundamental to success in university than the ability to write English prose. Start a serious program of reading now or, even better, yesterday. You say you don't like to read? Ah, well then.....

STUDY MATH – AND LEARN TO LIKE IT

Or at least study it. When we told you we were going to give you friendly and helpful advice, this didn't imply that it was advice you necessarily would welcome. Here it is: if you want a chance at the fullest range of careers after graduation, you must study mathematics at university, and this means taking serious math in high school, not the watered-down courses. We can hear the protests and howls of rage already. Canadian students, raised in an era of celebration of individual choice and encouragement of easy pathways to success, have learned to fear and hate mathematics. We will admit that high school math is often poorly taught — for lack of properly qualified teachers, more than one high school has assigned a physical education or English teacher to teach a math course. Nevertheless, math is one of the most important and foundational subjects in high school. If you intend to go to university and if you want a full chance at a wide range of careers, you must study academic math in high school. What is more, if you want a real shot at twenty-first-century success, you had better be reasonably good at it.

Let's start with the hardest sell, that math is intellectually challenging and fun. Properly taught, high school math is full of riddles, puzzles, creative formulas, and, most importantly, problem solving. Math teaches mental agility, builds a life-long facility with numbers, and provides a foundation for advanced study in other academic subjects. It is not easy — but neither is English for those who don't have a natural aptitude for it — and it is a program of study that is truly incremental: what you learn in elementary school is essential for high school, which in turn is a requirement for success at university. You have to study math, stick with it, internalize its intellectual dynamics, and learn to apply its thought processes if not its formulas in many other aspects of your life.

Many Canadian students are at a severe disadvantage compared to those of other nations (although, surprisingly, our performance on international tests suggests that, as a group, Canadian young people do reasonably well — tenth out of seventy countries in 2009, down from seventh three years earlier).[2] In East Asia (where attention to mathematics is an obsession) and in Eastern Europe, there is a deep commitment to the fundamentals of mathematics. All students study math throughout their school years. They learn by rote and they work in very competitive environments, their parents working as hard to push them on as most Canadian parents spend convincing their children they are all above average. By rote we mean, for instance, that they memorize the multiplication tables, something that many Canadian schools abandoned in favour of getting students to "understand" what eight times seven is.

The result of all this is that Canadian students, as a rule, develop a strong aversion to mathematics. Even Barbie got into the act. A few years back, one of the talking Barbies was programmed to say "I hate math," generating widespread anger among feminists for stereotyping young girls as being anti-math. Actually, boys hate it just as much. High school students and university students alike talk about math courses as the academic equivalent of a colonoscopy (if you don't know what a colonoscopy is, look it up, and be glad you are still young). Some persist, particularly the science-oriented, because they are told that studying math is good for them or because it's a program requirement. But the majority of the students opt out. Only a minority of high school graduates have taken advanced high school math — advanced meaning the kind that all collegiate graduates took two generations ago. Many of those who take it do so more than once, struggling to get the math scores that they need to get into the most competitive programs.

This leads to the practical reason for tackling mathematics. Students who do not complete the right high school courses and who do not succeed at first-year university math will find more than half of all the programs on campus closed to them. Some of the most popular academic and professional fields — engineering, applied science, finance, accounting, economics, computer science, environmental modelling — require a high level of fluency in and comfort with math. In other areas, math is included as a barrier and test, a program requirement that does a fine job of weeding out the weak and unmotivated from the hard-working and determined. Check the program requirements across campus at the university closest to you and see what programs require high school and university math.

Equally important, those programs with high math requirements are also the programs with the greatest career opportunities and the best income levels for graduates. Without math you could be denying yourself access to some neat and interesting programs. Career-wise, you will be blocking access to the best-paying and highest-demand jobs in the modern economy. The message is simple. Study math. Work hard in high school and try to enjoy it, and if you can't enjoy it, work hard anyway. If you can't warm to it, then study it because it is essential to your future and will determine your options in university and, very likely, in the workforce. If you say "but I hate it," we won't say "suck it up," but that's what we are thinking....

HOW ELSE SHOULD YOU PREPARE?

Beyond the two major things (learning to write and studying math), the things that you need to do to succeed in university — or wherever else you may go — are largely evident through common sense and open dialogue with parents, teachers, and people working in whatever job appeals to you. Nevertheless, we'll note the following pieces of advice:

- If you're going to university, you should take the high school courses that prepare you for post-secondary education. Take the serious math courses, not the easy ones designed to make sure that every eighteen-year-old, no matter how unskilled, has a high school diploma. Take the serious English courses, the ones where you have to read Shakespeare (*please* tell us that your school offers them), not the so-called "applied" ones with names like "Contemporary English" or "Communications." It's true that there are some universities in Canada that will accept any grade twelve course for admission, but you don't want to go that route.

- Construct a résumé that will indicate what a stellar person you are, as well as giving you as much practical experience as possible. Do what interests you: coach a young kids' soccer team, be a camp counsellor in the summer, teach Sunday School, win a prize at the Science Fair, or learn to play the bassoon. Don't just loaf around texting your friends and following Justin Bieber on Twitter.

Everything positive you do adds up, and when you are applying for a university program that's hard to get into, your impressive résumé will be a big help. Good luck.

CHAPTER TWELVE
SURVIVING AND THRIVING
IN POST-SECONDARY EDUCATION

GETTING SETTLED IN NEW SURROUNDINGS

Let's assume that you have made the jump and decided to go to university (the largest group of you), college (the second largest) or a polytech (a smaller number but growing fast). Hopefully, you've done the work necessary to determine which path is right for you and then completed the preparatory work that we outlined in the previous chapter. Now you've just been dropped off at your new residence, have boarded a bus to a campus far from home, or are setting up study space in your parents' basement. So, what's next? What do you have to look forward to? How can you best adjust to a strange and challenging environment?

The three types of institutions named above are not the same, and their programs differ greatly. Small, elite programs pay a great deal more attention to you than mass-enrollment, first-year courses at big universities. Small campuses are more welcoming. College, on the other hand, is more like high school — particularly if you attend the one close to home. Expect to see some of the high school crowd, smallish classes, and much less intensity than at a university. Polytechs are like universities, but with higher energy and much more focus on applied and practical work. You will be doing things right away at a polytech and finding your feet more slowly at a university.

The advice that follows is fairly generic — although it applies best to the university and polytech environment and less so to colleges. The jump in standards and expectations is much greater between high school and university and polytechs than it is between high school and a college — depending, of course, on the particular program you are in. University campus life is more complex and all-encompassing than what you will find at a polytech or a college, with many more rituals, ceremonies, and traditions. But even that varies. A high-intensity polytech, like Sheridan, has much more of a buzz than an access-oriented university like York or the University of Toronto, Scarborough. If you've chosen to further your education at any of these places, dig in and have fun. Capitalize on opportunities, make new friends, participate in campus life, and absorb the intellectual and professional benefits of the place. You are off on a very different kind of adventure.

Here's a decision that will have a huge effect on your university experience: should you live at home — assuming that there is a university in your community — or should you go away somewhere and live in a university residence, or an off-campus apartment? We've had both experiences, since one of us did live at home as an undergraduate, while the other went to a university a long way from his home community. On the whole, we recommend going away, but there's no question that living at home is cheaper — assuming your parents don't charge you rent — and there's not as much of a break in your social life (something that has disadvantages too). But if you can possibly afford to do so, we think you should go to a different community and even a different province. We won't belabour this point here, since we make it in several places, but it's a decision that comes with choosing a university.

FINANCIALS

When it comes to the question of costs, you will read different estimates. Polytechs and colleges generally have lower fees for most programs — though these, too, are changing. Our estimates for universities are based on the online cost editor for McMaster University,[1] which is representative of Canadian universities outside Quebec. In Quebec, fees are much lower (but only for residents of the province, so if you are from Ontario, you can't save money by going to McGill). The basic tuition fee varies according to province; for McMaster it is about $6,500 a year for arts and science students and just under $9,000 for business students. Then there are various extra fees — such as compulsory student and athletic fees (McMaster includes them in the tuition figure). Residence costs also vary, but a double room with washroom is $5,400, and a meal plan is $3,135 (more for big eaters). McMaster reckons $1,200 for books (which seems hard to believe and, in fact, varies a lot between programs — but some science texts are amazingly expensive).

McMaster estimates $1,000 for "personal expenses" and $1,000 for "entertainment," which isn't very much spread over eight months; you'd have to live a pretty spartan life to get away with that. The total is over $18,000. The figure of $15,000 is often given in estimates of how much university costs, but given the breakdown on the McMaster website, the higher figure seems, if anything, rather low. Note that this does not include the cost of running a car; if you have one, you might spend $20,000 a year. If you finish in four years, you will have spent $80,000; if it takes you five, something that is quite common, you are looking at $100,000.

A hundred thousand dollars! It won't be any comfort to hear that, at the most expensive American universities, the cost of tuition and board alone has now passed $60,000 a year — as much as $300,000 for your degree! This is a sum that seems out of most peoples' reach, and is a reason that student debt is such a crushing burden in the United States. Even these days $100,000 is a great deal of money. It has to be paid too — the university won't release your transcript or let you graduate until you have paid every last penny. And, if you leave without a degree and owing money, they may put the debt collection agencies on your trail. Perhaps your parents have money in a RESP, but they are unlikely to have that much in it. Perhaps they are wealthy and can simply cut cheques every year — some are, and if this is the case, you are lucky. If you live at home for free, you can save about $8,500 a year — or something approaching half the total cost, which is a big reason why so many students do this.

Why, you ask, shouldn't the government pay for it? After all, your education is a benefit to society, especially if you are studying something useful and practical such as medicine or civil engineering. The traditional argument is that, even if you are studying something that is not particularly useful to society (say Latin and ancient Greek literature), your education makes you a better person, and this is to everyone's benefit. True enough, but the counter-argument is that your education also benefits you — because, on average (but only on average), it gives you a better salary than you would get without it. This isn't Cuba, where doctors make the same as street sweepers, so perhaps you should pay something up-front for your more prosperous future. Thirty years ago, governments paid about 80 percent of the cost of running universities; then they started shifting the burden to students, who now pay about half the total cost. Short of marching in the streets Quebec-style, this is not likely to change.

Perhaps you can get some financial help. Scholarships and bursaries are both money that the university or other sources give you; the difference between them is that the first are based on academic achievement, while the second are based on need. At McMaster, the university gives three levels of "Entrance Awards" to everyone based on high school averages, ranging from $500 for 80 percent to $1,000 at 90 percent. If you get 95 percent or more, a figure that would have been impossible in the baby boomer days unless you were a mathematician on the level of Stephen Hawking, but is more common now, the award is $2,500. There are also in-course scholarships, and other ones donated by outside groups that give awards to the children of veterans and the like.

Bursaries come with a wide requirement of sums and conditions, but generally go to students who demonstrate need. Ontario has an interesting one called the "First Generation Bursary" for students whose parents did not attend a post-secondary institution. There are all sorts of external bursaries, and it will certainly be to your advantage to do a thorough search for them. But unless you are an outstanding genius and win some sort of full-ride scholarship, you will still have to come up with a substantial amount of money. It may help to be an excellent athlete, since Canadian universities do, contrary to what most people think, give some financial help to star players. However, the limit a student athlete can receive in Ontario is $4,000,[2] which is why institutions in the northern American states are full of Canadians on hockey scholarships.

You are going to have to live on a budget. Sorry, we know that budgeting is a pain, but there's a big reason for doing it: you don't want to come out of university with a huge student debt if you can possibly avoid doing so. In 2012 half of graduating university students had debt, and the average amount for those who had it was $28,000.[3] This means that some students carried $10,000 in debt, and some more than $40,000. Our favourite horror story about student debt is the American woman who wanted all her life to be a veterinarian, so much so that she borrowed money to take her degree at an institution in the Caribbean. Now thirty and working at the Caring Hearts Animal Clinic in Gilbert, Arizona, she owes the American government $312,000, money that, unlike other debt, cannot be discharged in bankruptcy, and will dog her (sorry) all her life.[4] This won't happen to you, though, unless of course like her you take a degree at the Ross University School of Veterinary Medicine on the island of St. Kitts and borrow heavily to pay for it.

Unlike the American system, which will hound (sorry again) the vet forever, the Canadian system allows you to default on your student loan, and there are websites that advise students how to deal with financial difficulties. But you don't want to do this; it's a dog's life (blush), it's not very responsible, it's bad for your credit, and you will eventually want to borrow money to buy a house, something that's difficult to do if your credit rating is bad. Even if you pay the loan off on time, as most students do, it's no fun starting life owing $28,000 or more. You could buy a pretty nice car for that amount. This is no time to suffer the remorseless logic of compound interest.

You need to ask yourself how much you need a car, or an iPad — Android tablets are cheaper and just as good — or lots of other consumer items. If you have a student loan, everything you buy is essentially on credit, though admittedly at a much better rate than the credit card companies will give you. You have to have some fun — why not a ski trip to Whistler? — but you have to consider whether it's worth adding to your debt load. If, on the other hand, you have the money and are debt-free, then *laissez les bons temps rouler* (as long as your assignments are in on time).

It's also possible that your parents can't afford much help, you don't have a scholarship, you don't want to burden yourself with debt, and yet you want to go to university. How are you going to manage this? Traditionally, the answer was a summer job and, indeed, it used to be possible to make enough money between the first of May and Labour Day to pay tuition, books, and part of the room and board. Almost everyone could do this, and those with connections could get an industrial job that saw them come back to campus with a substantial amount of money. For some lucky students, this still works, but not many of you are going to find a job that pays $18,000 over the summer. You could, of course, get a full-time job for a year or more and save like a beaver for university expenses.

This takes a great deal of self-discipline, but some students do it, and it's a really good idea.

The usual answer to this is to take a part-time job. It used to be that poverty-stricken students would be hired by the university to wait on tables in the dining room and do similar jobs, but these are usually done by outside workers nowadays. The common solution is to get a job in a restaurant or bar (in the days when the drinking age was twenty-one, this was not possible). The statistics on this are startling: *Maclean's* magazine in January 2012 quoted a Canadian University Consortium study to the effect that 56 percent of students work for wages during the university year, an average of eighteen hours a week. Nearly a fifth of them work more than thirty hours.[5] That's twice as many hours tending bar as spent in class for a traditional five-course lecture-based program. Are you a student working in a bar — serving tables or tending bar — to the point where it seems as though you're taking classes in your spare time? Sometimes it's difficult to tell.

Pity the student who has to do this, who has to spend thirty or even forty hours working, for example, in the "Ceeps" (the CPR hotel in London, Ontario, favourite watering hole of Western students).[6] Add to this fifteen hours in class. University people say that you should plan to spend three hours working on a course for every hour of class time. For an arts program, with typically around fifteen classroom hours a week, this translates into a forty-five-hour-per-week commitment. For a heavy science program, add an extra ten to fifteen hours. And you haven't had any fun yet, to say nothing of sleep or social interaction. Somehow many students who figure that they can do a full course load and take on a full-time job wonder why things are not working out so well. This is the kind of pressure that makes students drop out of university, and is an important reason why so many take more than four years to finish their degree.

Worse still, such a work and study schedule leaves no time at all for one of the greatest things about being a university student, which is the opportunity to go off on trips of self-discovery. If you are in class or labs fifteen hours a week, and spend another thirty working on term papers, course readings and other assignments, and if you don't have an outside job, you have a huge amount of spare time to go and hear guest speakers, play touch football, join student organizations and clubs—the choir, the Society for Creative Anachronism, political organizations, charitable, and volunteer groups. Above all you have all that wonderful time to learn stuff outside of the classroom and outside of your required reading and assignments.

Why not choose the debt-free route? Yeah, yeah, you're thinking — easy for you guys to say. What's the answer? Where is the money to come from? Well, we can't prescribe for you, but what we would do in a situation where we had no money is not take out huge loans, and not kill ourselves and ruin the university experience by working ourselves ragged. What we would do is the third option suggested. We would take as much time off between high school and university as we needed to get together enough money to see us through the degree. You are going to have to pay the money back eventually; why not get it up-front and enjoy your university years? You may well have a better experience if you come to university at twenty-one instead of eighteen in any case.

> ## LEARNING OPPORTUNITIES BEYOND THE CLASSROOM
>
> There's the library, with hundreds of thousands or millions of books, depending on where you are, most of them unavailable on the Web. You can wander down the stacks and find interesting stuff that will grab your attention.
>
> Then there's the famous chemistry professor, Dr. Whatshisname, the Nobel Prize winner, lecturing to a class of graduate students. Perhaps you can slip in to the back of the class and listen to him. Here's David Suzuki or Ann Coulter giving a public lecture (well, not Coulter: the president of the University of Ottawa caved to pressure and banned her). Go and hear it.
>
> All this you can do if you aren't spending thirty hours a week slinging suds.

Give this some serious thought. You've been at school for twelve years, and you have four more to go in university. If you wait a couple of years and save your money you will have a far better university experience in every respect: you will be more mature, you will have more real world experience, and you won't have to wait on tables or serve beer in a pub. It's surprising that more young people don't do this. Perhaps they think that if they don't go to university at eighteen they will lose the will to go, and will never do so. But if the impulse is that weak, perhaps they weren't meant to go in the first place.

WHAT IS YOUR PLAN B?

We have noted elsewhere that only a very small minority of people who express interest in medicine actually get into medical school. (Of those who do get in, almost all graduate, because the entrance standards are so high that no one who gets in is incapable of doing the work.) It must be terribly disappointing to be rejected, especially for those who have been answering "doctor" to the question "what do you want to be when you grow up?" since they were old enough to talk. Some try more than once and do eventually get in. Others go to the kind of offshore medical school that landed that poor American vet $300,000 in hock to the government.

Some will go elsewhere in the medical field, into nursing or medical research, while some will go into other branches of science. Some will choose other fields entirely, and some will simply drop out. The point is that you need a plan B. Given the success rate for medical school applications it would be foolish to put yourself in a situation where you've invested two or more years in something that comes crashing down around your ears, leaving you with no idea of what to do next. One solution is to take courses that will be useful in medically related fields. For instance, business courses might help if you want to make a career in the pharmaceutical industry. Perhaps you could become a high school science teacher. In any case, don't leave yourself open to disaster like a deer caught in headlights. Plan for contingencies.

YOU'RE NOT IN HIGH SCHOOL ANYMORE

This seems obvious, but think about what it means. It means that you are now on your own in a number of ways. The most important of these is that, by and large, university instructors are not going to compel you to do anything. Most notably, very few of them take attendance, so that if you want to skip class, there is no immediate penalty. No bad conduct marks, no going to the principal's office, no detention, no expulsion. What freedom, and what a wonderful change from high school. You will find that the absence of the police/prison guard atmosphere that is so much a part of school life makes all the difference in the world. Being responsible for your own success (or failure) through self-discipline (or lack of it) is what distinguishes you as a young adult from the child you used to be not so many months ago.

But of course there's a corollary. If you don't come to class, and there are marks for class participation, you will get nothing. If you miss the deadline for handing in a term paper, you will be severely docked or will get nothing — unless the instructor is a pushover, as some of them are. If you skip labs, you will get nothing. You aren't in the Edmonton school system anymore, the one that decreed that teachers could not assign zero grades, even if students had done nothing at all, on ridiculously stupid pedagogical grounds. A hint, though, comes from the chair of the Edmonton school board, who said it was the board's policy "to entice students to perform as effectively as possible."[7] Entice — what a lovely word. Well, no one is going to entice you to complete course requirements at university. There they are, do them or not, and take the consequences. A bit scary, but liberating.

You have other new freedoms too. Assuming you are living in residence, you can sleep in as long as you like, party till dawn (assuming you don't break the noise regulations), change your clothes every day or never, eat residence food (everyone complains about it), drink and experiment with dodgy substances with no parents tut-tutting. Some people overdo aspects of this (see below on booze and drugs), some people make many friends, some people isolate themselves and are unhappy. It's up to you. No one will run your life for you. You're not in high school anymore.

STAY IN RESIDENCE, AND GET A ROOMMATE

Living in residence is more expensive than living with Mom and Dad, but we think that you should have the residence experience if you can possibly afford to do so. We don't think you should live in an off-campus apartment in the first couple of years; that can be a very isolating experience. In fact, some of the elite American universities, Duke for example, require all first-year students (they still call them freshmen) to live on campus in residence.

We make this recommendation for several reasons. An important one is that it gets you out of your parents' house. You are aware of the meme (an English-prof word that means an idea or belief that spreads through a culture) of the unemployed college graduate in his or her thirties still living in Mommy and Daddy's basement, an object of derision and scorn.

You don't want to end up that way (so you'd better start planning your future carefully right now), and really, the sooner you cut the umbilical cord, the better. Living at home prolongs your adolescence and delays your transition into adulthood. You don't want that, do you?

Naturally there will be exceptions. There are people who for cultural reasons will be more closely bound to their families, and will live at home till marriage, and thus would not dream of going to live in a university in a residence. There are others who for one reason or another need more family support than they will get living in a university residence. This advice is not directed at them.

You should get a roommate too; in fact, some universities will not put first-year students in single rooms. Your first reaction may be to say "but what if the roommate is loud/a drunk/annoying/a nerd/smelly, etc.?" If your roommate is truly horrible, abusive, or some sort of psycho, you can always ask to be moved — but the point is that part of your adult life is learning to get along with all kinds of people. You are a devout Christian, and your roommate is an atheist. You are an intellectual, and your roommate is a hockey jock. You are a neat freak, and your roommate is a slob, or vice versa. How are you going to get through the year? Well, that's the whole point: you are going to have to find some way of getting through it — with patience, accommodation, or negotiation.

You really want to get away from the "helicopter parent" situation, so called because these people hover over their university-aged "children" like search-and-rescue helicopters over crash victims. They register for their children in their children's names; they phone the registrar's office to see how their kids are doing (by law, the office can't give out information). They phone the instructors to ask why their kids didn't get an A on their last term paper. Unbelievable, you say. But it's true, and it's getting more common all the time. Do you want to stay at home and be smothered in that way?

There are new friends to be made in residence. Some people who live with their parents while at university tend to hang around with the old high school crowd, people who are living with their own parents. In a university residence you will make not only new friends, but ones from a much greater variety of backgrounds than your old neighbourhood. This is valuable not only as a means of broadening your circle of friends and your horizons generally, but also as a great means of making contacts that will be useful in your later life. Imagine that you are in the business program, and down the hall in residence is a student whose father is a vice-president of the Bank of Montreal. You are interested in art, and your roommate's mother is a conservator at the National Gallery of Canada. What a terrific resource! Such things happen more often than you would think, particularly at the higher-rated universities.

Not only should you live in residence, but you should seriously consider asking to room with an international student. This is one of these win-win situations where you do a good deed but get a big reward in return. The good deed part is obvious: a great many international students are seriously deficient in English, especially spoken English, despite having taken English as a Second Language courses. They are just as adrift in Canada as you would be in Punjab with only a shaky knowledge of Punjabi. Everything about Canada is strange to them, and some of it is frightening. Imagine coming direct from Amritsar to Saskatoon, especially if you start in January.

You can do a really good deed and get lots of good karma (as your grandparents used to say) by helping a student like this navigate a strange and new country. Some international students hang around exclusively with students from their own country, which is a really bad idea — most importantly because it reduces their chance to practise English with native speakers. If they room with you, they will have no choice but to speak English, though you may learn some Punjabi or Urdu or Cantonese as well.

But there's something in this for you too, other than good karma. Remember why you are at university. We hope you are there to broaden your horizons and learn as much as you can about the world. Some students are, while others are just there for job reasons. Getting to know a student from another country really well is a tremendously broadening experience, especially if you are from a part of the country without a large immigrant population. But even from a more practical perspective, becoming a good friend of someone from, say, Hong Kong or Japan can have all sorts of benefits. Wouldn't it be fun to spend a year or two in a Japanese or a Chinese city learning the language and working as an intern for some commercial firm, or teaching? Think of all the benefits that might flow from this. If your roommate isn't able to help you in this, he or she may know someone who can. Doesn't this sound more interesting than going back to your home town and teaching elementary school at the same place you went to? You can always do that later if you really want to — and, in any case, there's a huge oversupply of teachers these days and it's really tough to get a job.

DON'T BLOW OFF ORIENTATION

Almost all universities have an "orientation week" in which first-time students are given tours of the facilities, with talks by academic, residence, and student activities administrators. Of course your eyes may roll at the thought of someone walking you through the library, but it's worth taking the tour. Libraries are much different than they were twenty years ago, when they were simply repositories for huge numbers of books and periodicals. The old file-card cabinets have been replaced by computer terminals, and the people behind the desks are highly computer-savvy, able to direct you to valuable online resources that you will need in your research. It's good to know where the health services office is before you need it, how the cafeteria system works, what the student government can do for you, what the residence rules are, what athletic facilities are available (some places have amazing facilities that rival those of the fanciest health club), and so on. All this is well worth the time you spend on it.

If you are in residence, you can use these days to get to know your roommate. If he or she is truly awful, you can switch, though the residence authorities are reluctant to do this, and are likely to ask you to give the situation some time. This is when you get to know people who may end up being your friends for life, and it is a serious mistake to skip this period and come to campus the day before classes start. We won't guarantee that every moment of orientation will be golden: the person who gives the little talk on how the university's grading system works may be a total bore. But, on the whole, orientation is very much worthwhile. Don't blow it off.

TIME MANAGEMENT: SELF-MANAGED LEARNING

You will hear about this during orientation, but it bears repeating: time management is essential for success at university, and it is vitally important that you pay attention from the first day of classes onward with regards to how you spend your time. Very few of you did this in high school, but this is another place where university is different from what went before: you absolutely cannot afford to goof off during the academic year. The best thing to do is to get a day-timer — a calendar where you keep track of what you are doing — so that you won't forget when your classes are, and when your assignments are due. You can get paper ones, but probably a good digital one would be best or just make use of your smartphone's calendar app, if you have one. We assume everyone has a laptop; ten years ago very few of you did, but times change, and a computer and smartphone are now essential. You should set aside a certain time of the day for study, and plan ahead for a big push for assignments of various kinds.

You need to know what you are doing for the week ahead, day by day, and for the month ahead, and for the whole semester. You should allocate your time as though you were getting paid by the hour. Of course you want to socialize, but you have to set aside time for study as a priority.

We know some eyes will roll at this advice. You think it's nerdy to have a day-timer like some compulsive high school dweeb sucking up for grades. Certainly if you are at university just to party, or to kill time, and you don't care about grades, you shouldn't bother. If you are working in a pub forty hours a week we don't really know what to say to you, since you probably have every minute of the week allocated already. But you have to realize, though we've said it several times already, that Canadian universities are swarming with students, most of them aiming at the kind of career you want, and there are not nearly enough places in these careers for all who want them. Therefore it is essential that you take every step possible to distinguish yourself from the swarm.

The point of time management is to arrange things so that you do your best possible work. To lose grades because you are rushed on your assignments is a great shame, and will have a bad effect on your academic and work career. Be aware, too, that the first month is the most important one, so you need to take it seriously from the first day.

Our favourite piece of advice for students is to make the first month of every academic year work for you. We focus on this first month for two reasons. First, because focusing on the first month generates real results. Second, because very close to 100 percent of all students ignore the suggestion. You will arrive in school in early September. The first few days will be taken up with orientation. Smart students will take the academic part of it seriously and go easy on the social, boozy part. Then classes begin.

Most students take a full load of five semester-long classes, each with its own set of classes, seminars, labs, readings, and assignments. The course syllabi you collect the first week are quite daunting but, hey, you have four months, so what's the worry? The answer is that there is a lot to worry about. Here is what most students do — they procrastinate. No one is watching and monitoring your progress. Few professors provided much scheduling advice. A few smart or lucky students will be in residences with mentor dons who can guide them through the perils of first year, but the majority will be on their own.

As you go through the course assignments, you will see a bunch of essays, projects, reports, and summaries that you have to do. Even if you were reasonably conscientious in high school, you actually have no idea of how long it takes to write a university-standard assignment, which the professor says must be 3,000 words long and have at least fifteen academic sources. (By the way, it's a very bad idea to use Wikipedia as an academic source in university assignments. It's wonderful for looking up facts, but unreliable for modern contentious subjects — the entry on George W. Bush used to change every day — and using it will make your instructors think you are a lightweight.)

But, what the heck, that is only one paper. There is also, of course, the psychology mid-term, the three English papers (each requiring you to read a novel or play first), four biology lab reports and a mid-term, and the weekly assignments in first-year German. Some classes require weekly readings. One of us taught a semester at an American university where senior history classes required students to read 250 pages a week, and they were quizzed and graded in class on their reading. Work stacks up — that is the bad news — but it is all down the line — and that's the really bad news.

SURVIVING AND THRIVING IN POST-SECONDARY EDUCATION **191**

Most first-year students procrastinate. They put off their assignments until, in a mad rush, they struggle to cope with mid-term examinations and essays and reports and other work — all in the second half of the semester. The first half, meanwhile, has been left largely work-free. This pattern is as predictable as a Saskatchewan winter, with students panicking in late October and early November, requesting extensions (most profs say no, though some softies will give you one), pulling "all-nighters" in a desperate attempt to keep up with deadline (a really bad idea: how clearly do you think at 3 a.m.?), and watching their grade point average plummet in a flurry of poorly written essays and mediocre projects. The library, largely empty in September, is swarming with students in mid-semester, many of them frantically searching for the same books.

The solution is so elegant and so easy that it is remarkable more students do not adopt this strategy. Well, actually, it's not that remarkable, since it runs against most people's basic instincts to put tasks off. Start your assignments early. Go through all of the work that you have to do in the semester. Determine which essays or reports can be done right away and which ones have to be done at specific times in the course. Do as many of the assignments as you can in September. The library will be largely empty. The books and materials you want will be on the shelves. Librarians and writing centre staff have lots of time to help you. You are not otherwise busy. Get at the least the first draft done right away. You can always go back and revise the papers closer to the deadlines.

Following this advice will set you on a manageable path to academic success (assuming that the essays are properly written and researched). You will avoid the post-Thanksgiving panic, your work will be more carefully presented, you will experience much less stress than your classmates, and you might even be able to enjoy the work. Ignoring this advice, and we know that the swarm will do so, will leave you with a very relaxed six-week period, followed by an intense and stressful second half of the semester. Most students never quite get the logic of this approach, continuing the pattern of coasting and crisis semester after semester

So, take this as the first test of your ability to respond to good advice. Tackle your first-semester work like a military campaign. Plan ahead, develop a workable strategy, apply yourself early, work consistently, and capitalize on the full semester's worth of time and opportunity. But we

THE MATHEMATICS OF FIRST-YEAR ASSIGNMENTS

You will have x number of papers to write. The papers will, on average, take you y number of hours (and y is about three times larger than what you did in high school, because you can't just make it all up out of your head, like a story — you have to substantiate your facts through research). Make note of this and plan accordingly.

You must, therefore, find xy hours in order to complete your assignments over the course of three months. You can spread this out over all of September to early December (the smart way to operate) or you can delay starting your work and cram it all into the last six weeks of the semester — the standard modus operandi for first-year students. But these students are the swarm, and you don't want to be part of that, do you?

smile as we write this. If we have learned anything from watching students over the years, it is that you do not, as a group, plan very well, are not strategic in your approach to university life, and somehow believe that a panic-stricken race to complete ten assignments in three weeks will miraculously produce top-notch work. Big sigh.

Don't skip classes, even the boring ones (and some will be so boring that you will want to drive spikes into your ears — we would be lying to you if we told you that all your instructors will be excellent). We are thinking of non-science courses now — but, of course, you won't skip labs if you are in science. In lecture courses, take notes that are as extensive as possible. They can be useful for study, and in our undergraduate days we found that if we wrote down as much as we could, it helped us to remember the material, and made studying for exams much easier. For heaven's sake, if you are going to bring a laptop to class, don't search Facebook on it. Either use it for note-taking, or turn it off. If you are surfing the Web, you will annoy the instructor, and for all the good the class will do you, you might as well have stayed in bed.

MAKING THE MOST OF THE FIRST YEAR

In most programs you will have some choice of courses and, as well as taking the courses you will need to get into the major of your choice, you should seriously consider taking one course a semester in a field you know little about. This is a great way of deciding on a field you want to concentrate on for the rest of your undergraduate career. We don't mean that Arts students should take organic chemistry, but they might consider a course in an area they have never studied: sociology, psychology, natural resources, and so forth. Scope them out first, because you have to balance taking courses that will interest you and challenge you against the necessity of keeping your grades up. If taking a course in, say, ancient Egyptology sounds like a grade killer, you can audit it, usually for half the course fee, or just slip in and listen to some of the lectures. Maybe you will get turned on by the difference between hieroglyphic and demotic script and make it your life's work. You will never know if you don't sample.

Here are a few other ways to make the most of your first and other years:

> **HOW'D YOU LIKE TO TRADE PLACES WITH US?**
>
> You know something? Talking about this with you in this way is making us a little envious.
>
> You are going to have a great time at university if you take the right steps to prepare yourself. We wish that we could follow you to campus as young students once again, especially now that we know how to make the system work.
>
> Tell you what: let's switch roles — you be old geezers, and we'll take your place, draw up a study schedule, join some clubs, go out for the track team, and yes, have a great social life (we'll get to that shortly). What do you say? Fair trade?

- **Attend public events.** When politicians or other famous people come to campus, go and listen to their public lectures. Subscribe to a newspaper online. Hang around the library and read some magazines for free. Find out what you like. All of this is possible because you have taken our advice and are not working in a bar thirty or forty hours a week; you have all that time to hear a lecture on the Rosetta Stone, listen to Naomi Klein, and read *Scientific American*.

- **Get involved in intramural activities.** Because you have followed our advice, you have time for them. Intramural sports (from the Latin "within the walls," that is, not with other universities) exist in every conceivable form, from touch football to field hockey to fencing. Political organizations run from conservative to far-left progressive; if you want to shock your parents, you can join the Communists. Join a volunteer organization; become a Big Brother or Big Sister, and do this because it's a good thing to do, not (just) because it will look good on your résumé. Just don't do all these things at once; you don't have *that* much time.

- **Be smart about your social life.** You're going to have to cut us some slack here, because we are old guys talking to young people about romance and sex (not always the same thing, by any means), alcohol, and drugs. There's a danger that anything we say on these subjects will sound hopelessly out of date or, even worse, creepy. Nonetheless, who you are as a sexual and social being — that is, establishing your sense of sexual identity, engaging in romantic relationships, choosing when and how much alcohol you consume, and deciding whether or not you will take recreational drugs — most often matures during your post-secondary years. There are two fundamental rules when it comes to sexuality and relation- ships: the first — especially in this time of HIV, AIDS, and various STDs — is "play it safe;" the second — which should be obvious and can apply to issues beyond human sexuality — is "be a decent person." Sex, love, and possibly commitment are always in the air on university campuses. Be aware of this fact and make the most of it, always remembering the two rules. When it comes to alcohol and drugs, pragmatism needs to lead the way. As you know, alcohol poisoning is a very real thing, and illicit drug use is, beyond being illegal, simply a very good way to destroy both brain cells and aca- demic records. The philosopher Democritus (Greek, 460–370 BCE) said that "immoderate desire is the mark of a child, not a man." Good advice.

GRADE SHOCK

We end this chapter with some news that might dismay you: studies have shown that the majority of first-year students at university get worse grades than they did in their last year of high school, sometimes much worse. A July 2010 study in *Maclean's* published some alarming statistics: approximately 75 percent of students get lower grades than they got in high school. Of these, two-thirds go down one grade (the average drop is ten points from, say, A- to B-), and one-third drop by two letter grades (for example from A- to C-). Around 25 percent do about the same as in high school; and only a tiny minority, under 3 percent, see their grades improve.

The resulting shock can be great. Here you were an honours student in high school, and you are now just a B student or worse. How embarrassing, how worrying for your parents. Sometimes this affects your finances too, for some scholarships depend on keeping your grades up. The good news, though, is that in most cases this does not mean your intelligence has drained out of your ears during that last happy summer after high school graduation. It is simply a reflection of the absurd grade inflation that has poisoned the integrity of the Canadian high school system over the past forty years. Two generations ago there was a fair correlation between high school and university grades, but once the schools adopted a "student-centered" system of education, grades started to rise. If you doubt this, we will give you one statistic. Ontario awards the title "Ontario Scholar" to any high school graduate with an 80 percent average. When this began, in the late 1950s, fewer than 4 percent of graduates were Ontario Scholars, and they were awarded $400. Two years ago, almost half of graduates got 80 percent (and there's no money anymore).

Universities have adjusted accordingly. In 1990, the average grade of students entering UBC was 70 percent; in 2000 it was 80 percent; and now it's close to 90 percent — not because students are any smarter, or even because UBC has raised its standards, but because high school grades keep floating ever skywards. Some more elite programs, such as the Desautels Faculty of Management at McGill, now require around 90 percent, not as an average, but as a floor for admission. This issue shouldn't affect you except to serve as a warning that high school grades have no guaranteed relation to university grades. However, if you are capable and work conscientiously, you should do all right. Just don't expect straight A grades with minimal effort.

So, be warned and be prepared. University is to high school as army boot camp is to summer camp at the lake. You will be treated like an adult from the outset, even though many first-ear students are not ready for the challenge. Close to 30 percent of all first-year students drop out or fail out. Welcome to a tough world.

CHAPTER THIRTEEN
WHO ARE YOU
AND WHAT ARE YOUR CHOICES?

WHICH OF THESE PROFILES BEST DESCRIBES YOU?

By now you should have a pretty good idea about who you are and which of the options we have outlined in this book has the best chance of helping you achieve a prosperous and interesting life. No one ever fits exactly into a category — but there are some general patterns that do make sense. You know much of this now: if you are curious, university is a good bet. If you like to work with your hands, an apprenticeship program can be great.

So, to wind up this long lecture, here is a rough guide to various profiles of young people, with suggestions for which options might best suit them. As always, we want you to be honest with yourself as you consider where you might best belong. This definitely is no place for cheating on yourself.

THE SEEKER

You are looking for deeper meaning in life, beyond money and career, are smart, intelligent, highly motivated, but don't know what to do with your potential. Thank goodness for you. The world needs more like you, people who care deeply about the environment, social justice, and spirituality. Take time to define your place in Canada and the world. A year of travel and volunteering could help a lot. If you are religious, Bible colleges provide excellent opportunities for personal and spiritual development — and many are good academically as well. So, take the time to explore — the world, your options, and your place in society — and give yourself the time to build the skills you need to make a difference with your life. Volunteer with a not-for-profit organization and discover some of the thousands of people out there who share your passion for making the world a better place.

THE SWARM MEMBER

You know who you are. You are not a reader, do not write much, do not particularly like school, plod along with average grades, lack motivation, and have no idea what you want to do in life. You are going with the flow, following your classmates into college and university prep classes, looking into the same schools as your friends, and tuning out parents and teachers when they talk about the need to raise your game. You are undeservedly confident and may be heading for a real crash. You can get into university or college if you decide to go, but remember that that is no great accomplishment these days. In many ways, we wrote this book for you. You are the kind of student who sits in the back of the first-year lecture hall, rarely does the reading, hands in mediocre assignments, and looks terminally bored by the whole college or university experience. You are — not to mince words — not ready for the big time. You need time to mature, develop a focus in life, and decide what you want to make of yourself. There is no "royal road" out there, no employers waiting to offer you jobs at $60,000 a year. You might muddle your way through university; but you will likely crash and burn on the job hunt. Your boredom and casualness are serious turn-offs to would-be employees, who have their radar set for underachievers like you. You really need a reset. You need to consider all of the options we have laid out here and you need to slow down your rush through life. You need to prove yourself, through volunteering, work, or business — and you need to find your purpose in life. Trust us.

THE BRAIN

You are really smart and hard-working, you love to read, and you are ambitious. Head to university and consider the professions, including medicine. Realize that you will have many options in life, and be open to exploring new possibilities as they emerge throughout your studies.

Remember, too, that at university you will not likely stand out from the crowd as much as you did at high school. You are the one that universities love to teach. But there is no easy route to real success, and many of you will experience two disconcerting things: your grades may drop, often substantially, and some people who finished behind you in high school will soar to the front of the class. So here's a warning. If you had to work like a beaver to get top grades in high school, you may be in for a shock. University is much harder. Students who worked moderately hard at their schoolwork and did lots of other things make the best university students. Obsessive students often have trouble adjusting to the more free-form system at university. So, turn on the afterburners.

THE THINKER

You are intelligent, love to read, have strong writing skills, but are not strong in math or science. Too bad. You should have worked harder and sooner on the math and science, for you have narrowed your university and polytechnic options considerably. No degree in civil engineering for you! But there are many good opportunities for you — including law, teaching, and government service. These days, too many of you are heading into business, but give serious thoughts to an arts program as well. People like you, if they are really good and willing to work hard, can succeed anywhere — in business too. You should follow your instincts about university, taking a broad first-year program and looking for a field of study that really interests you.

THE BUILDER

You are good with your hands and like to make things, but you are a non-reader — that is, you rarely pick up a book, magazine, or newspaper to read for pleasure. If you did reasonably well in high school, you are probably being pushed toward university. Pay attention to the warning signs: non-readers do not do well in university. There are great options out there, but you should probably focus on the polytechs, colleges, or apprenticeships — or spend some time in the workforce before you take the plunge. Remember that there's good money in the skilled trades. Many of you will do very well in life, and could easily out-earn a lot of those heading directly to university. Surprise yourself. Surprise everyone.

THE WAFFLER

You are reasonably smart, you lack specific goals — but you like money and the good life. You are a candidate for the swarm, but are academically better than most of that group. You are one of those being directed toward university, even though your heart is not really in it. If you have entrepreneurial skills you may be okay, as long as you have a strong work ethic. But you could have a difficult future, and the first year in post-secondary education could be a real shock. We are worried about you. Take some time off — volunteer, work, and get your act together. You can go to college, polytech, or university if you are really committed, but you will be wasting your time if you are not prepared to make a life change in doing so. Remember, you are in danger of becoming a swarm member, of falling into the undifferentiated mass that is heading into a career and financial desert. This is your chance to stop waffling and decide that you are going to exploit all of the talent and ability that you possess. Nothing less will do.

THE TECHIE

You are smart, reliable, hard-working, inventive, but non-bookish. You are well suited for the polytech alternative. Colleges and apprenticeship programs are other good options. But even here, know that the best opportunities will go to people who read. You have great opportunities ahead and the business world is really looking for people like you. But start reading more. Become a real specialist in areas that you find interesting and make sure you get some work experience. In the current economy, you have surprisingly good opportunities, but you have to apply yourself — harder than ever — if you want the best ones.

THE REACHER

You come from a disadvantaged family background. You have not been treated fairly in life, and have discovered that the system does not really cut you a lot of slack for poverty, family circumstances, isolation, and other challenges. You have probably faced many struggles in your youth, but you are intelligent and willing to work hard to get ahead. Many of you, particularly from single-parent families, have an inspiring parent pushing you on. You may be unaware of the real opportunities available for you and likely underestimate your skills and options. We worry about you, mostly because you are likely to undersell yourself. Rich kids do better than you in school, but you are probably every bit as smart and talented. Seek out a trusted teacher, a counsellor, or a community mentor — and pay close attention. They have a better sense of your potential than you do. Don't let anyone — including yourself — sell you short. We admire you for seeking to capitalize on your basic abilities. By the way, there is a fair bit of assistance, financial and otherwise, from community groups, colleges, polytechs, and universities for people in your situation.

THE RICH KID

You have enormous advantages, great social skills, and a healthy sense of entitlement. While your parents' money may buffer you from most of the realities of life, we are worried about you too. Money can get you a car and all sorts of electronic gizmos, but it cannot write your examinations, get you to work on time, or motivate you. Take the best lessons from your parents and their friends — entrepreneurship, drive, ambition, work ethic, and, yes, money — but realize that you need to be your own person. Dump the sense of entitlement; there are no easy paths to achievement. Capitalize on your privilege, and realize that you can make a difference in the world. Consider taking some time to volunteer. You could probably do with a reality check about how the rest of the world lives. We've met a lot of you at universities over the years. You came to complain about your grades, and some of you had your parents call in to support your case. Tacky. And counterproductive. It is devastating to fail when your parents have given you so many advantages — but it is possible, and painful to watch. Buckle down and prove yourself.

THE HIGH SCHOOL HERO

There are adults who see high school as the best years of their lives. You may be a high school athlete or campus leader — with great social skills and a reasonable academic record — but you feel seriously unsure about the future. You must know that very few of you are going on to become professional athletes. In our world, the best ones are marked for greatness in their early teens. Being the best athlete in a mid-sized regional high school might not even put you in the top hundred in your province. So, what now? If you are a good athlete — and, surprisingly, the best opportunities may be in the smaller sports, such as gymnastics, golf, or diving — look into athletic scholarships, including in the United States, where they are more generous. American colleges have great deals — up to free tuition and room and board — for top athletes. Canadian colleges, polytechs, and universities offer a lot less money, but they generally support their athletes well (often better than the general student population). If you truly love your sport, even if it will not be a full career, why not ride it as far as you can? If you don't know what you want to do career-wise, consider taking a year off to work, travel, or volunteer. You need to put the cheering crowds and high school heroics behind you and focus on your career and educational prospects.

THE TIGER MOM SURVIVOR

You have intense parents. You have done well in school and have high grades and an impressive list of accomplishments. Your parents have been on your case since elementary school, insisting on music lessons, extra-curricular homework (don't you love Kumon, Oxford, and the Sylvan Learning Centres?), volunteer activities, and a sport or two. They have driven you mercilessly, and you are tired of the lack of free time and the control exerted by your parents. Take the time to give your folks a big hug and a great "thank you." You are better prepared than most for what lies ahead. Sure they pushed you — to be ready for a harsh, competitive world where the advantages go to the most intense and highly motivated people. You have real potential at university, polytech, or college. Don't resent what your parents did to and for you. In the years to come, you will discover how much better prepared you were for adulthood than your classmates who were coddled and spoiled by their parents. But speak frankly to them about what you want. While they often have fixed ideas — medicine, law, accounting — about what you should do, many will change their minds if you show you have done your homework. If that doesn't work, consider drawing a teacher or guidance counsellor into the conversation.

THE CHALLENGE SURVIVOR

An increasing number of students with serious learning difficulties and mental health issues are making it through high school and even through college and university by virtue of enormously hard work and parental devotion. These are people who, two generations ago, would have been simply sidelined — and we heartily applaud them for their achievements. Only those young people wrestling with these challenges — and their parents and siblings, of course — understand in full the frustrations, difficulties, and effort required to succeed. Our elementary and secondary schools have many more supports than in the past, providing young people with a platform upon which they can build a choice of futures. Post-secondary institutions provide similar assistance, and many more students are overcoming psychological or other barriers to learning. Our country is much the better for their determination. They may face other challenges with the transition to the workplace. We think, though, that if you can master the world of post-secondary education, you can probably master anything, and we have no fears for your future. Good for you. Do not, however, assume that the next stages will be easy or automatic, as there are significant barriers to advancement still in place. The work ethic and sheer guts you needed to move forward, however, have likely prepared you well for the difficult issues of the workforce.

THE REST

These profiles cover the great majority of Canadian high school graduates. Simple categories, of course, never cover everyone. There are other groups — Stoners, Drop-Outs, Juvenile Delinquents — who face real challenges in the coming years. Some of you — are you reading this book? — were ill-served by being kept in high school until you were eighteen years old. You would have been far better off getting some work experience — and a jolt of reality — starting at sixteen. Too bad that government makes this route so difficult. If you are in this category you will need to make a strong effort to succeed in life. But it can be done, and we urge you to do it. Someone in this category who reads and can write reasonably well can recover and find good opportunities down the road. Ditto those with technical skills, from car mechanics to computer programmers. Most of you, particularly those with behavioural or social issues, need time to grow into your brain. While your classmates are facing difficult choices at seventeen and eighteen, you will have your turn ten years later. When the time is right, colleges are great places to relaunch yourself, and apprenticeships can serve very nicely if you are technically minded. Like it or not, you are going to have time off now, probably to find a job of some sort. Life is not over at eighteen — not by a long shot. Surprise yourself, your parents, and your classmates. You can make a lot of your life — but it will take hard work. You are part of a large group in Canada — and government, business and the education system are seriously worried about you. Unless you, collectively, get your act together, this country could be in serious difficulty.

A FINAL NOTE TO STUDENTS

In the end, the decision about the future is really up to you. Parents are influential, and so are teachers. They have your best interests at heart, but they are not going to live the rest of your life for you. Don't underestimate the importance of the choice you are about to make. There are tens of thousands of dollars in immediate costs involved — and a career of earning and opportunity waiting to be defined.

We know it's hard. Life is like that — awkward, complicated, unnerving, and very, very real. You are about to become an adult — and we know that the prospect is scarier than most of you are prepared to admit. There are no easy paths ahead. Hard work, curiosity, intelligence, integrity, and character will ultimately matter more than whatever credential you end up with. Welcome to the reality of the twenty-first century. It *is* a jungle out there, with no easy path and no obvious choices. If we have alerted you to the wide range of possibilities and convinced you to take this post-high school decision very seriously, we have done our job. Over to you.

A FINAL NOTE TO PARENTS

We have been rough on you. We are parents, and grandparents too. These have been hard decades to be a parent, with the pressures of economic uncertainty, popular culture, drugs, teenage sexuality, and on and on. Oh, for the easier times of our youth, right? But North American parenting has been a significant part of the problem facing our children. Many parents have been permissive, and have given their children everything they possibly could want — probably too much and too soon. We bought into the cult of self-esteem, without realizing that telling our children they can be all they want to be is hokum. (Did that work for you? Great if it did — but Ken dreamed of being a major league baseball player and that plan never made it past Babe Ruth League.) The global economy has been tough. You know this, in your own lives and in those of friends and neighbours around you. And you want what is best for your kids. We get that.

But be wary of following the crowd, of assuming that the *learning = earning* mantra of our age actually means something. You need to help your children get the right opportunities, not the popular ones. If they are truly ready for university, then prepare them for it, save money (and make them pay part of the cost), and support them in their exploration of campuses and programs. Try not to impose your will on them. Instead, focus on encouraging them to keep their options open rather than narrow their vision to a single degree. Make sure they keep up their math and science in high school, support a broad first-year program so that they can explore post-secondary opportunities, go with them to visit colleges, universities, or polytechs. If they are uncertain, do not rush them. A year of work, travel, or volunteering could do them a world of good.

Your greatest challenge is going to be letting go. Your children are young adults. They have to become independent-minded, even if that means making mistakes and suffering broken dreams. Congratulations on getting your sons or daughters through to high school graduation. While academically this is not the challenge it once was, socially it is a much harder task than in the past. A complex, ever-changing world awaits them. You have done your very best to get them ready.

* * *

We want to end by returning to a point we have made repeatedly. To students: try to avoid going with the flow — what we've called the swarm. In our new world, specialization and differentiation matter much more than being part of the crowd that, lemming-like, may be heading for the employment and career cliff. Canada's system of colleges, polytechs, universities, and apprenticeship programs provides many avenues for personal development. Work, entrepreneurship, volunteering, and travel add to the range of options. To parents: your children — your young adults — need the ability to navigate the world on their own, and on their own terms. Support them in this vital journey, even if it takes a markedly different path than you had anticipated. Their future is not going to be the same as our past. If we are lucky, it will be even better, with more opportunities and additional benefits. But, finally, it is their world, not yours, or ours. It is our duty to launch them on their way. From this point on, they are in control.

NOTES

INTRODUCTION

1. That is, we'll try to sound like we're giving the advice you'd get from a friendly uncle who has your best interests at heart.

CHAPTER 1

1. See our article "The $1 Million Promise," *Maclean's*, January 21, 2013.

2. Zach Weiner, *Saturday Morning Breakfast Cereal*, n.d., *http://www. smbc-comics.com/index.php?db=comics&id=2729#comic*.

3. The Conference Board of Canada reported that 88.4 percent of adult Canadians had completed high school as of 2010, which ranked the country second out of seventeen "peer countries." The United States has a slightly higher rate. See Conference Board of Canada, *How Canada Performs: High-School Completion*, March 2013, *http://www. conferenceboard.ca/hcp/details/education/high-school-graduation-rate. aspx*. Statistics Canada reported that 89.5 percent of Canadians between the ages of 20 and 24 were high school graduates in 2009–10 (Kathryn McMullen and Jason Gilmore, *A Note on High School Graduation and School Attendance, by Age and Province, 2009/2010*, November 3, 2010, *http://www.statcan.gc.ca/pub/81-004-x/2010004/article/11360-eng.htm*).

4. In the 1990s shares of Bre-X, a penny-stock mining company, soared on claims of a massive gold find in the Indonesian jungle. When these claims turned out to be fraudulent, the stock collapsed. A capsule

summary of this notorious Canadian scam can be found at Sam Ro, "BRE-X: Inside the $6 Billion Gold Fraud that Shocked the Mining Industry," *Business Insider*, July 1, 2012, *http://www.businessinsider. com/bre-x-6-billion-gold-fraud-indonesia-2012-7*.

CHAPTER 2

1. Council of Ontario Universities, *Applications & Enrolment: Information about the Number of Students Who Attend Our Universities*, February 23, 2013, *http://www.cou.on.ca/applications-enrolment*.

2. The figure for taxi drivers is from Mark Trumbull, "Have Degree, Driving Cab: Nearly Half of College Grads Are Overqualified," *Christian Science Monitor*, January 28, 2013, *http://www.csmonitor. com/Business/2013/0128/Have-degree-driving-cab-Nearly-half-of-college-grads-are-overqualified*. In 1970 it was 1 per cent.

3. On the subject of post-secondary education for firefighters in the United States, see Paul Fain, "Advanced Degrees for Fire Chiefs," Inside Higher Ed, October 27, 2011, *http://www.insidehighered.com/news/2011/10/27/college-degrees-increasingly-help-firefighters-get-ahead*.

4. The American National Retail Federation (*http://www.nrf.com/modules. php?name=Pages&sp_id=1245*) says that 49.5 per cent of retail workers "have college degrees, are currently in college, or have attended college."

CHAPTER 3

1. You read *1984* in high school, right?

2. "10 Reasons to Do a Gap Year," *http://www.studentawards.com/stacks/articles/10-reasons-to-do-a-gap-year.aspx*.

3. Statistics Canada, *Table 2: Postsecondary Status of Young Adults Aged 24 to 26 by December 2005, by Province and Type of Institution Attended*, November 17, 2008, *http://www.statcan.gc.ca/pub/81-595-m/2008070/t/6000011-eng.htm*, shows dropout rates by province. Quebec's is the lowest, but that's because dropouts there take place at the CEGEP stage, not at university.

CHAPTER 4

1. National Association of Career Colleges, *Active Members*, *http://www. nacc.ca/w_active_members.aspx?#selectedSchoolBox2237*.

2. Canadian Information Centre for International Credentials, *Private Career and Vocational Colleges in Canada*, *http://www.cicic.ca/417/ Private_Career_Colleges.canada*.

CHAPTER 10

1. The chart is available at Ellis Chart: Comparative Chart of Apprentice Training Programs, *http://www.ellischart.ca*. It's named for Frank Ellis, the director of apprenticeship in Saskatchewan who first developed it.

CHAPTER 11

1. See Ken S. Coates and Bill Morrison, *Campus Confidential: 100 Startling Things You Don't Know about Canada's Universities* (Toronto: Lorimer, 2011), chapter 7, "Your Grades Will Drop."

2. "Canada Slipping in Math, Science and Reading Skills," *Postmedia News*, December 7, 2010.

CHAPTER 12

1. McMaster University, *Cost Estimator*, *http://future.mcmaster.ca/money-matters/cost-estimator*.

2. Ontario University Athletics, *http://oua.ca/sports/2011/7/15/Student%20 Financial%20Awards.aspx*.

3. Historical statistics on tuition fees and student debt levels are available online from Statistics Canada.

4. Shannon Doyne, "What Investment Are You Willing to Make to Get Your Dream Job?", *New York Times*, The Learning Network, February 25, 2013, *http://learning.blogs.nytimes.com/2013/02/25/what-investment-are-you-willing-to-make-to-get-your-dream-job/?partner=rss&emc=rss*.

5. Jacob Serebrin, "More Students Balance School with Jobs," *Macleans. ca* on Campus, January 25, 2012, *http://oncampus.macleans.ca/educa tion/2012/01/25/more-students-balancing-school-and-part-time-jobs/*.

6. For some boozy nostalgia, see L. George and Barry Wells, "Sucking Back the Suds at the Ceeps Since 1890," *http://www.altlondon.org/ article.php?story=20090901180023187*.

7. Edmonton *Sun*, March 19, 2013. The policy has since been modified to permit the possibility of zeros.

INDEX

PRAISE FOR THE AUTHORS' WRITING

"A BRACING REALITY CHECK THAT SHOULD BE ESSENTIAL READING FOR ... ANYONE WHO THINKS HIGHER EDUCATION HOLDS ALL THE ANSWERS."

—MARGARET WENTE, *GLOBE AND MAIL* COLUMNIST

So you're thinking of going to university.

No doubt your parents and teachers have made it clear that getting a degree is the best way to ensure that you get a good job. Or maybe you already have a B.A. or B.Sc., and now you're thinking of going back to enrol in a law school, business program, or teachers college. That should guarantee you a better position than the one you have now. Right?

With youth unemployment at record levels, there are no longer any sure bets. Will there be a job for you in the knowledge economy when you graduate in four years? Will the coming flood of teacher retirements open up opportunities for you? Will there still be jobs for engineers in five years' time? No one is certain.

In this unstable environment, it's hard for you to plan for a secure future. Let Ken Coates and Bill Morrison help you explore the diverse opportunities and career paths that are open to you in Canada. They will help you decide whether to pursue an undergraduate degree, enrol for skills training, or investigate one of the many other options that are available.

KEN S. COATES has been a university administrator for more than twenty years. He is also a prolific author, whose titles include *Canada's Colonies*, *The Modern North*, *North to Alaska*, and many academic books. He is currently a Canada Research Chair in Regional Innovation at the Johnson-Shoyama Graduate School of Public Policy, University of Saskatchewan. He lives in Saskatoon.

BILL MORRISON was a professor and administrator at universities in Ontario, Manitoba, and British Columbia and a visiting professor in the United States before he retired in 2010. Morrison has published fourteen books, twelve of them in collaboration with Ken Coates. He lives in Ladysmith, BC.

 DUNDURN

 $24.99 | £16.00

ISBN: 9781459722989

9 781459 722989